Politics and the Crisis of 1860

UNIVERSITY OF ILLINOIS PRESS, URBANA, 1961

Politics

and the
Crisis of 1860

WILLIAM E. BARINGER

AVERY CRAVEN

DON E. FEHRENBACHER

NORMAN A. GRAEBNER

ROBERT W. JOHANNSEN

Edited by Norman A. Graebner

To
ROBERT L. FORTENBAUGH
In Memoriam

Preface

In November, 1860, the New Orleans *Delta* responded to the news of Abraham Lincoln's election to the American presidency with a warning of the South's impending doom:

The announcement of the result of the election of yesterday, and triumph of the party whose declared purpose and policy are to undermine the very foundation of the prosperity, safety, and existence of the Southern section of the Union, has thrown a pall over our city, and filled all minds with deep anxiety and gloom.

Men, parties and partisan traditions must alike be consigned to oblivion. Our homes, our firesides, our social system, our honor, our liberty are enough to engage our undivided affection, care, solicitude and devotion. The South must consult, deliberate and determine with the grave dignity and serious purpose of a people who stand on the brink of a great peril—who are compelled to choose between a dishonorable submission and capitulation to a haughty and uncompromising enemy, for a temporary peace and the security of certain material interests, with an ever present and increasing peril to even these, or accept all responsibility, danger and honor of a united resistance at all costs and sacrifices, to the dishonor and eventual ruin which are inevitable from our acquiescence in the Government of the fanatics and sectional demagogues to whom the Northern masses have committed the powers of this Government.

Historians for a century have attempted to explain this Southern mood, for to understand it is to understand the Civil War. Whatever the nature of the sectional conflict of the fifties, it had reached the stage by 1860 where the election of a Republican to the White House would cause some Southerners at least to regard their vital interests threatened with destruction. Eventually their fears would drive them to seek their future welfare and security in a Southern Confederacy rather than in a Republican-dominated Union. Lincoln's victory suggested that thereafter things would be different, but no one, least of all the secessionist leaders, spelled out precisely how the election challenged the continued existence of Southern civilization. Herein lies the puzzle of the South's reaction. Was the Republican Party a threat to Southern institutions? If so, what was the character of the threat? If there was no clear and immediate danger in Lincoln's election, why did the South attempt to escape the leadership of a Republican president even at the price of secession? To suggest answers to such critical questions as these is the purpose of this small volume.

These five essays, commemorating the centennial of the first Lincoln election, were presented originally at the fourth annual Civil War Conference at Gettysburg College in November, 1960. Each of these essays accepts the verdict that by the campaign of 1860 some form of crisis was inevitable. Nowhere do they insist that all choices had been eliminated except those which the North and South followed. But they agree that the nation had reached an impasse from which it could no longer escape without some measure of violence. The conflict had become irrepressible. On the central question of why and how this occurred, those who contributed to this volume have presented a variety of answers.

Concerned broadly with the issues and events of the campaign, these essays dwell emphatically on the importance of slavery to the sectional conflict and to its impact on American politics. As Lincoln was to observe during the Civil War, "Without the institution of slavery, and the colored race as a basis, the war could not have an existence." Slavery accounted for the vast revolution in American politics during the fifties, especially the rise of the Republican Party and the eventual disruption of the Democracy. Don E. Fehrenbacher and I agree that the success of the antislavery movement in Northern politics, especially after the introduction of the Kansas-Nebraska Bill in 1854, resulted from the fear engendered by the notion that a slave power threatened to overrun the nation and destroy the free institutions of the North. It was this fear that led to the concept of total conflict and reduced the struggle to one between freedom and slavery. The nation, in Lincoln's words, could not exist half slave and half free. Eventually one would triumph over the other. Yet this concept of an aggressive slavocracy, so essential for the ultimate triumph of the Republican Party, raises the question of sincerity among antislavery politicians, for obviously the vast majority of Northern Democrats and old-line Northern Whigs never regarded slavery a threat to their section at all.

Republican campaigning by 1860 created the impression that time was running out—that the struggle between freedom and slavery had to be resolved promptly in one way or another. Republican orators made it clear that freedom was not to be the loser. Southern civilization, they warned, would not survive a Republican victory. Yet the South was no more prepared to concede its slave structure in 1860 than it had been a decade earlier. It was not only the heavy investment in slaves that bound the South to its slave labor system; it was also the conviction that slavery alone guaranteed a tranquil social and political relationship between whites and Negroes in the South. For secessionists the only choice remaining after Lincoln's election was that of submitting to some modification of the slave system or withdrawing from the Union. Inside the Union, ran their conclusion, slavery's days were numbered.

In this conviction, held by extremists in North and South alike, lay the irrepressible conflict of 1860. How the nation became trapped in this inescapable time of resolution is not clear. In my introductory essay I have assigned the conflict to the dichotomy between the antislavery attitudes of the North and the total absence of means for achieving the liberation of the slave. Neither the antislavery politicians nor the Southern secessionists pursued objectives that could be resolved within the context of the American political and Constitutional system. Yet neither group could retreat from its demands on the other without destroying the political symbols which it had created. Such a dilemma could be resolved only with violence. When that would occur depended on the "occasion."

Fehrenbacher finds the irrepressible conflict in the

Southern fear of the growing power of the Republican Party and in the resulting conclusion that Lincoln's election "carried with it the implication of that society's doom," although he makes it clear that the Republican Party was no immediate threat to the South. Robert W. Johannsen discovers the irrepressible conflict within the Democratic Party itself—in the uncompromisable discrepancy between Northern and Southern Democratic views toward slavery expansion. Rather than concede their claims to equality in the territories, Southern leaders, having anchored their political futures to this principle, favored secession as a final political maneuver against the North.

Avery Craven attributes the central conflict to the apparent pressure on slavery itself, suggesting that it turned on what the North said, not on what it had done. He insists, however, that the Republican threat was not limited to its alliance with the antislavery forces of the North, but included also its alliance with the Modern World which seemed capable of sweeping everything, including the Southern slave economy, before it. The Republican Party, responding to Northern interests as much as Northern ideals, was no conspiracy to destroy slavery. Citing the arguments of Southern moderates, William E. Baringer agrees with Craven that the Southerners attributed too much power to words. But the moderates, whatever the superior accuracy of their judgments of Northern power and the Northern determination to uproot the civilization of the South, failed to capture the Southern mind.

All five of us wish to express our gratitude to the officials and staff of Gettysburg College, especially to President Willard S. Paul, Professor Robert L. Bloom, and Mr. Raymond S. Davis, for their contribution to the success of the conference. These essays were improved by the presence and criticisms of such scholars as Ollinger Crenshaw, Wood Gray, Philip S. Klein, and David S. Sparks, who also participated in the conference. These lectures, as the conference itself, are dedicated to Professor Robert L. Fortenbaugh, for many years a member of the Gettysburg College faculty and the primary organizer of the Gettysburg Civil War Conferences, who died several months before the 1960 conference took place.

Urbana, Illinois   Norman A. Graebner
March 1, 1961

Contents

NORMAN A. GRAEBNER

I

The Politicians and Slavery

On September 16, 1859, the New York *Times* cautioned its readers: "It is time that we should begin to see whither the country is to drift in the approaching national canvass. . . ." Everywhere thoughtful Americans sensed a burgeoning crisis. In the words of William H. Seward the nation was locked in an "irrepressible conflict" between the invincible forces of Northern capitalism and the "slave power." Slavery, he warned the South, must give way inevitably "to the salutary instructions of economy, and to the ripening influence of humanity." With undisguised impatience Northerners chided the South for perpetuating an anachronistic and immoral institution in defiance of the liberal tendencies of the age. For some Republicans, confident of victory in 1860, the sectional conflict was approaching the time of decision. Whatever was unique in Southern civilization, they predicted, would not survive the economic and moral pressures of a triumphant and united North.

Southerners discovered consequences no less revolutionary in the political tendencies of the decade. To Jefferson Davis of Mississippi the Republican challenge was relentless as well as alarming. "It is no longer the clamor of a noisy fanaticism," he wrote, "but the steady advance of a self-sustaining power to the goal of unlimited supremacy." For others the threat was more specific. "The question before the country is the extinction of slavery," ran the conclusion of one Southerner. "No man of common sense, who is not prepared to surrender the situation with the safety and independence of the South, can doubt that the time for action has come—now or never!" At issue was the South's future in a Republican-dominated Union.

This simple notion that a Republican victory in 1860 would throw the South into full retreat and endanger its institutions underlay the nation's mood of impending disaster. Yet on the eve of the critical campaign there was no clear relationship between the North's moral purpose of liberating the slaves and its power to achieve this enlightened objective. That Northern reformers had launched a crusade against slavery appeared logical enough, for this institution dwarfed all other challenges to the fulfillment of an American democratic and moral order. Other social evils had been mitigated, if not removed, through individual and group action. Yet as an object of reform, slavery was totally unique in the nation's experience. What distinguished it from other social evils was not its magnitude, but its total integration into the legal, economic, and social institutions of the South.

Slavery enjoyed the protection of local laws under the guarantees of the United States Constitution. For

Henry Clay this fact alone made slavery, at least for his age, an irremediable as well as an unfortunate human relationship. In his noted speech of November, 1847, delivered at Lexington, Kentucky, he reminded the North: "Every State has the supreme, uncontrolled, and exclusive power to decide for itself whether slavery shall cease or continue within its limits, without any exterior intervention from any quarter." Even Abraham Lincoln recognized not only the South's Constitutional right to slavery but also its right to the return of fugitive slaves, for the latter, too, rested on long-established practice. In his famous Cooper Union address of February, 1860, Lincoln asked the nation to accept the judgments of the past which tolerated and protected slavery to the extent that its actual presence made that a necessity. "Let all the guaranties those fathers gave it," he said, "be, not grudgingly, but fully and fairly maintained."

Slavery, moreover, was an economic institution involving an investment of millions and a social institution completely submerged in questions of race. It was the racial contrast between master and slave that made slavery possible on American soil. On the other hand, the slave relationship alone appeared capable of guaranteeing the security and safety of both races in a biracial society. In those regions of the South where Negroes outnumbered the whites, emancipation threatened every aspect of the established political, economic, and social order. Where Negroes were not numerous, even Southerners admitted occasionally, a system of gradual emancipation might permit a peaceful transition toward freedom and protect simultaneously the interests of both races.

Obviously the slaveholders of the South, assured the

protection of governments which they controlled, would permit alterations in the legal structure of Southern society only if such changes contributed to their own advantage. The injustice of slavery itself, even if acknowledged by men of the South, suggested no remedy for the injustice. Henry Clay, for example, deplored the existence of slavery in the nation, but he resigned himself to its continuance. Slavery, he explained, was "a lesser evil than the frightful consequences which might ensue from the vain endeavor to repair it." Similarly William Medill, the noted Governor of Ohio, reminded a group of British abolitionists in October, 1853, "Gentlemen, I am as much opposed to slavery as you are . . . but as a nation we cannot get rid of it." For him the reason lay less in Constitutional barriers than in the existence of racial prejudice so deep and unreasonable that it left no legitimate place for freedmen in either Northern or Southern society.

Indeed, on the eve of the 1860 campaign the question of means remained the unresolved challenge of the antislavery crusade. For the abolitionists, slavery was a moral issue to be resolved through the individual regeneration of Southern slaveholders. These men were evangelists, not statesmen. "Our enterprise," Wendell Phillips once observed, "is eminently a religious one, dependent for success entirely on the religious sentiment of the people." But beyond their vehement and sometimes vituperative exhortation that the slaveholders stop their sinning, the abolitionists had no program for the South.

Such thoughtful antislavery philosophers as the Unitarian clergyman, William Ellery Channing, rebuked the abolitionists for undermining their own cause. Channing accused them of overemphasizing the evils of Southern civilization, dwelling on the slaveholders rather than on the institution of slavery itself, and threatening to destroy the community in which the slave existed. Such aggressiveness merely placed the South on the defensive and wedded it ever more firmly to its slaveholding system. Channing, who confronted the question of slavery's future as thoughtfully as any American, warned his fellow Northerners that emancipation would require such complex social and racial adjustments that it could proceed satisfactorily only on Southern terms. "Slavery ought to be discussed," he admonished. "We ought to think, feel, speak, and write about it. But whatever we do in regard to it should be done with a deep feeling of responsibility, and so done as not to put in jeopardy the peace of the Slave-holding States."

Channing saw clearly that the North possessed no greater power to destroy slavery in the South than it had to uproot social and political evils in foreign countries. But as the nation had the right and obligation to exert moral pressure against evils abroad, so the North had the right and obligation to challenge the existence of slavery in the nation. Channing assumed a rational world in which men sought what was right, not what was profitable. And in a rational world the "calm, firm assertion of great principles" would not fail. "The world is governed much more by opinion than by laws," he wrote. "It is not the judgment of courts, but the moral judgment of individuals and masses of men, which is the chief wall of defense round property and life. With the progress of society, this power of opinion is taking the place of arms. Rulers are more and more anxious to stand acquitted before their peers and the human race. National honour, once in the keeping of the soldier, is understood more and more to rest on the character of nations."

Unfortunately American society, no less than world politics, was governed more by conflicting interests than by abstract principles, and the material interests of slaveholders did not conform to the moral sentiments of the North. There existed no possibility that slavery could be exorcised by appeals to virtue. What gave the continuing debate over slavery its tragic quality was the vast dichotomy between the burgeoning demands for liberation of the slave and the inability of Northern writers, editors, and politicians to transform such demands into meaningful national action.

II

This absence of means rendered slavery novel among political issues. If the moralist of the forties and fifties required no more of himself and of society than the pursuit of individual regeneration, the politician faced the obligation to wield political power in resolving whatever public questions he might embrace. Clearly those challenges to national ideals which could not be allayed through governmental action had no legitimate place in politics, for there could be no relationship between the expanding pressure for national performance, as revealed at the polls, and the creation of policy itself.

This significant dilemma did not prevent Northern activists from resorting to political organization in their effort to expand the American antislavery movement. That slavery became a pivotal issue in national politics resulted partially from the conviction that the moral influence of the North might take strength from the sheer numbers espousing the antislavery cause, partially from the desire to reap the political rewards of an aggravated hostility toward the South and its institutions.

Although the Liberty Party gathered slight numerical strength as a third party in 1840 and 1844, it soon held the balance of power in several Northern states where the Democratic and Whig parties were almost equal in voting power. By the mid-forties, in the key antislavery districts of New England, New York, and Ohio, spokesmen of the old parties began to outbid the Liberty men for the anti-slavery vote. But nowhere did the antislavery politicians present a program of political action that could achieve their goal of universal freedom. The Liberty platform of 1844, for example, condemned the Federal Government for protecting slavery in the District of Columbia and per-petuating the Fugitive Slave Law. It accused Southerners of dictating the policies of both national parties, of filling Federal offices with slaveholders, and of denying the right of petition in Congress. It urged its adherents to "organize for efficient action" until "despotism shall have been driven from its last entrenchment, and thanksgivings for victory in the second great struggle for Liberty and Inde-pendence shall be heard throughout the land." Unfor-tunately the party gave no indication what "efficient action" would achieve the objectives of its platform.

Hatred was a powerful emotion, and for an abolition-ist minority it alone was sufficient to arouse and direct great energy. But hatred of slavery had its limitations as a political force. Most Northerners could sustain no mood of deep antagonism toward men they had never met or institutions they had never seen. They were concerned primarily with the satisfaction of their own wants. They would oppose slavery when it threatened their opportunities or their way of life. They would react when their own freedom was involved. Until then slavery was remote, like an abscess on somebody else's foot.

Western farmers, leading free and prosperous lives, had no interest in a perplexing and apparently irremediable problem that comprised no barrier to their material gain. Abolition, they feared, would simply flood the North with free Negroes. Conservative businessmen of the Northeast, with their heavy investments in Southern cotton and commerce, avoided antislavery politicians as being a threat to their estate. But between these two groups stood the rising middle class of the Northern cities—the true spokesmen of Northern economic progress—in hard pursuit of opportunity and resentful of those who stood in the way. Here were men of wealth in search of leadership and a program that would unlock the doors to an expanding future. They had few emotional or economic ties to the South; their markets and raw materials were in the North. The antislavery movement might never influence their emotions, but it might appeal to their material interests if they were ever convinced that slavery stood in the path of their progress.

Ultimately the successful exploitation of antislavery sentiment in American politics emanated from the conviction that slavery represented a political power that could be checked only through the creation of a countering political force. The movement, in short, took its strength from the notion that a slave power was reaching beyond the confines of the South through its influence over the Federal Government. For antislavery politicians, therefore, victory would come when they had transferred, either by intent or by accident, the concept of slavery's confining influence from the Negroes of the South to the farmers, merchants, and industrialists of the North. This required, above all, the effective identification of all dangers to the country's welfare with an immoral institution and with immoral concepts of society that, by the accident of geography, lay neatly segregated in one portion of the nation. It required the instructing of Northern men to find their enemies, not at home in opposing philosophies or party structures, but in another section where they could always be identified by their ownership of slaves. Through such techniques antislavery politicians would war against the extreme multiplicity of American political behavior and drive all issues into a sectional mold that would bipolarize the nation politically, reduce the South to its minority status by weakening its political affiliations in the North, and eventually permit those who controlled the North to control the nation as well.

Northern politicians inaugurated this process of sectionalizing national issues when they attributed the economic stagnation of the early forties to the actions of the Southern aristocrats. In December, 1840, for example, local antislavery leaders informed a group of wheat farmers near Akron, Ohio, that they would not resolve their plight until they sent men to Washington who would cease taking orders from the cotton plutocracy. Early in 1841, Joshua R. Giddings, the indomitable abolitionist Whig of Ohio's Western Reserve, accused the Federal Government of squandering Northern funds for the purchase of bloodhounds, not to wage war on the Seminoles of Florida, but to track down runaway slaves. Slavery, ran this expanding theme, was simply draining the North of much of its wealth without returning any compensating advantage. The Liberty Party platform of 1844 not only attributed to slavery the "impoverished and embarrassed condition" of the slave states but also charged the institution with having a "withering and impoverishing effect" on the free states. "Slavery," declared Joshua Leavitt, the noted abolitionist, "has been the prime cause of all the financial tornadoes which have swept over our country. . . . It is a bottomless gulf of extravagance and thriftlessness."

Giddings, above all other antislavery politicians, recognized the economic implications in the move to annex Texas. He warned the House of Representatives in May, 1844, that if Texas were admitted to the Union, its delegates to Congress would hold the balance of power. He reminded his colleagues that the tariff and river and harbor improvements were the key issues before the country. Was the North prepared to deliver these policies to the people of Texas? "Are the liberty-loving democrats of Pennsylvania ready to give up the tariff," he asked, "to strike off all protection from the articles of iron and coal and other productions of that State, in order to purchase a slave market for their neighbors who . . . breed men for the market like oxen for the shambles?" Would Western Democrats, he added, willingly give up "their harbor improvements, and the improvement of our river navigation, for the purpose of improving the southern slave trade, and of perpetuating slavery in Texas?"

By 1846 no important measure could pass Congress without provoking a sectional assault. Giddings accused the South of supporting the Oregon compromise only to defend its slave system. It was for this reason, he said, that it had feared war with England: "They see before them the black regiments of the West Indian Islands landed upon their shores. They now call to mind the declarations of British statesmen, that 'a war with the United States will be a war of emancipation.' " Giddings had predicted that President James K. Polk, a Tennessean, would eventually support compromise to save the institution of slavery. Such charges reduced the Oregon Treaty of June, 1846, to a matter of Southern dictation.

Polk's economic measures were attacked even more violently as evidence of Southern control of all national policies. In a narrow party alignment, the vote of the two Texas Senators carried the tariff reduction of 1846. As the Pennsylvania protectionist press poured forth abuse on the national administration, Northerners everywhere could recall Giddings' warning against Texas annexation. Polk's veto of the River and Harbor Bill, with its special provisions for the improvement of navigation on the Great Lakes, seemed the administration's final rebuke to the economic interests of the North and Northwest. Most Southerners had voted against the measure and created the impression that Southern pressure was responsible for the veto. One Chicago editor wrote: "The North can and will be no longer hoodwinked. If no measures for protection and improvement of anything Northern or Western are to be suffered by our Southern masters, a signal revolution will inevitably ensue. . . . The fiat has gone forth—Southern rule is at an end." The *Daily Sanduskian* complained bitterly that "we have an administration that knows no country but the South, and pursues no object but the perpetuation of slavery."

III

In confronting the nation with the question of national expansion, Polk's Mexican policies added a new and disturbing dimension to the concept of an aggressive slavocracy. The slavocrats, charged the administration's antislavery critics, had started their career of enlarging the area under their control with the annexation of Texas. Now the diabolical conspiracy of slaveholders had forced a war on Mexico to extend slavery into free Mexican territory reaching to the Pacific. The *Ohio State Journal* declared in May, 1846: "The administration, in attempting to consummate a scheme for the extension and strengthening of Slavery and the Slave Power, had involved the country in a War, which the people are now compelled to take off its hands and prosecute." Slavery was responsible for the debasement of the country, for the murder of thousands of helpless Mexicans. To prevent the further expansion of slavery, David Wilmot, the little-known Representative in Congress from Bradford County, Pennsylvania, offered to the House in August, 1846, a proviso that "neither slavery nor involuntary servitude" should ever exist in any territory acquired from Mexico, "except for crime, whereof the party shall first be duly convicted." The Wilmot Proviso became the symbol of Northern opposition to slavery's new assault on the Federal Government.

National expansion provided the antislavery politicians an unprecedented advantage. Now the slavocracy, already troublesome enough, threatened to enlarge its power at the expense of the North. The Wilmot Proviso alone stood between the aggressive slavocracy and the achievement of its expansionist ambitions. Even more important, the Proviso gave the North a conservative objective and freed it from the limitations imposed by the Constitutional guarantees of slavery in the South. It twisted the antislavery issue into a form that could more easily touch Northern self-interest, if not the Northern conscience. Abolitionism offered salvation to the slave; to its adherents it offered nothing but the rewards of virtue. The Wilmot Proviso offered nothing to the slave; to its potential adherents—the farmers, laborers, and capitalists of the North—it offered the opportunities of new lands free from the competition of slaveholders. Wilmot himself gave the new creed a distinct appeal when he declared: "I would preserve for free white labor a fair country, a rich inheritance, where the sons of toil, of my own race and color, can live without the disgrace which association with negro slavery brings upon free labor."

This Northern maneuver to stop slavery in its tracks culminated in the free-soil movement of 1848. At Buffalo, in August, an enthusiastic throng of antislavery leaders, representing all parties and thoroughly conditioned to the charges of Southern aggression, launched the new Free Soil Party. The Buffalo platform voiced the party's determination to rescue the Federal Government from the control of the slave power. Its program for achieving this goal was inherent in the charge "THAT IT IS THE DUTY OF THE FEDERAL GOVERNMENT TO RELIEVE ITSELF FROM ALL RESPONSIBILITY FOR THE EXISTENCE OR CONTINUANCE OF SLAVERY WHEREVER THAT GOVERNMENT POSSESS CONSTITUTIONAL POWER TO LEGISLATE ON THAT SUBJECT, AND IS THUS RESPONSIBLE FOR ITS EXISTENCE."

During the 1848 campaign many Free Soilers went

far beyond the platform's assurance that the party would not interfere with slavery within the limits of any state. For them the issue was no longer that of containing slavery in the South, but that of freeing the nation completely of its curse. "Our cause is the cause of our country—of the world—of humanity. It must triumph," said one Ohio editor. But the victory over slavery was demanded less by the needs of the oppressed slaves than by the danger which the slave power posed for the North and its free institutions. It seemed clear to antislavery editors that continued coexistence with slavery would result in the total degradation of the nation. As long as the slavocracy existed, the North seemed incapable of resisting its encroachments. For the editor of the Cleveland *True Democrat* the issue had been reduced to one of total victory or total defeat. "The greatest battle ever fought on American soil takes place tomorrow," he wrote on November 6. "It is between Liberty and Slavery." Yet the promise of a Northern victory was inherent in the fundamental weakness of the slave system itself. Indeed, the assurance of an ultimate triumph for freedom lay in the North's power to contain slavery within the Southern states. The institution would begin to die, explained the *True Democrat,* the moment its extension was prevented. By such doctrine the North held in its hands the means not only to destroy slavery in the nation but also to achieve that objective without defying the Constitution or resorting to violence.

During the early fifties antislavery politics came upon hard times. The Compromise of 1850, which disposed of the issue of slavery's expansion, destroyed the illusion of an all-conquering slavocracy. The South's acceptance of the principle of limited power in the territories eliminated the element of fear from the antislavery crusade. The Compromise, in reassuring the North that it could co-exist peacefully and profitably with the South within the confines of the American democratic process, split the purely free-soil from the more radical antislavery bloc in the North. It sent the moderate anti-Southern groups of 1848 scurrying back into the Whig and Democratic organizations, and compelled the genuine antislavery forces to retreat again to the single issue of abolitionism—an issue in which the vast majority of Northerners had no interest at all. If the Free Democracy perpetuated the third-party movement in the North, it was totally isolated from the main currents of Northern opinion. Those politicians whose futures hinged on their success in maintaining a broad antislavery coalition required nothing less than an issue which would resurrect the illusion of an aggressive slave power.

Stephen A. Douglas' Kansas-Nebraska Bill of 1854, which substituted the principle of popular sovereignty for the Missouri Compromise line in the Louisiana Purchase, provided the antislavery politicians two advantages which they did not possess in 1848. First, the fact that the alleged assault on free territory was led by a Northern Democrat from Illinois created the notion that Southern ideology had successfully infiltrated the North. Now the North was battling not only an aggressive slavocracy but also traitors in its own midst. Second, the struggle for power in the territories had been transferred from the remote deserts and mountains of the Southwest to the almost contiguous and reputedly rich agricultural lands of Kansas. Never before had the concept of an all-powerful South been brought home so clearly to the people of the North.

As the Cleveland *Leader* pointed out in May, 1854: "Nothing of less monstrous character could have opened the heavy eyes and dull ears of the North, to the objects and ends of the slave power."

In January, 1854, Senator Salmon P. Chase of Ohio and his antislavery colleagues, whose political careers were threatened by the mood of moderation that had swept the country after the Compromise of 1850, gave meaning to the North's incipient fears in their *Appeal of the Independent Democrats in Congress to the People of the United States.* "We appeal to the people," they wrote. "We warn you that the dearest interests of freedom and the Union are in imminent peril. . . . We tell you that the safety of the Union can only be insured by the full recognition of the just claims of freedom and man. The Union was formed to establish justice, and secure the blessings of liberty. When it fails to accomplish these ends, it will be worthless; and when it becomes worthless, it cannot long endure."

Such charges that the slave power was threatening the entire structure of free institutions in the North drove countless numbers of well-meaning Northerners into fusion movements from Maine to Illinois which captured the electorate in 1854. Within two years these fusionist groups had solidified to form the Republican Party.

Charles Sumner's violent and emotion-laden speech of May, 1856, turned Kansas into the political symbol required for the ultimate triumph of the new Republican Party. His dissertation on "The Crime Against Kansas" established the course of future sectional conflict. Its heavy emphasis on the evils of slavery revealed fully his abolitionist convictions and appealed to those who decried the existence of slavery anywhere. But the application of his hatred for slavery to Kansas and not to the South placed him firmly in the camp of the free soilers who, if they had little concern for slavery in the South, were determined to keep the territories free. Free soilism, with its broader appeal, remained the dominant issue before the country, but Sumner, in charging the Kansas question with high emotion, gave free soilism a moral foundation which it had never achieved in the late forties when the regions under debate were the distant territories of the Mexican Cession. Thereafter free soilism would gather strength from abolitionist sentiment, for the greater the hatred of slavery in the North, the greater would be the North's determination to limit its expansion.

Republican success hinged on the conviction that only a North united on the principle of freedom could stop the spread and ultimate triumph of slavery. During the campaign of 1856 the party spokesmen dwelt on the evidence of Southern aggression—the assault of Representative Preston Brooks of South Carolina on Sumner in the Senate chamber and the alleged sacking of Lawrence, Kansas, by Missouri "border ruffians." Republican orators even accused the national Democratic Party of attempting to establish slavery in Kansas under the subterfuge of popular sovereignty. True antislavery editors and politicians chided those Republicans who attempted to limit the party's program to free soilism. The Cleveland *Leader* warned in May, 1856: "It is impossible for freedom and slavery to exist together, one of them must be driven to the wall."

The Republican platform of 1856 declared it the duty of Congress to prohibit in the territories the twin relics of barbarism—polygamy and slavery. As a concession to the radicals it contained no reference to the Missouri Compromise. George W. Julian, Indiana's anti-slavery spokesman, commented on the platform: "I think I can stand on it, and without doing much violence to the language, preach the whole anti-slavery gospel. The restoration of the Missouri Compromise line is finally gathered among the defunct political humbugs of the day."

In the Dred Scott decision of 1857 the North suffered another humiliating blow, for this decision extended to slavery in the territories the protection of the Constitution. Thereafter even free soilism comprised a radical rather than a conservative program. Oliver Morton complained to the Republican state convention of Indiana in March, 1858, that the proslavery forces of the country had now captured the Supreme Court and deprived the North of any claim to the territories. That spring the debate on the Kansas Lecompton Constitution, which to Northerners defied the principle of popular sovereignty, seemed to prove that the South had captured the national administration as well as a hard core of Northern Democrats in Congress. Actually the Lecompton Constitution was an anomaly, for it was the creation of a proslavery convention which, because of prior disagreement on the question of submission to the Kansas voters, the anti-slavery majority refused to attend. Thus the Lecompton convention, although chosen democratically, did not reflect the views toward slavery of the vast majority of the people of Kansas.

Both the Dred Scott decision and the Lecompton debate rendered Kansas the battleground where the struggle against the slave power would be won or lost. "The year of 1858," observed the Indianapolis *State Journal,* "will see the great battle of freedom on the floor of Congress, on the plains of Kansas, where it will be decided whether a ruthless minority of southern slave-holders shall force a diabolical constitution on the free people of Kansas. . . ."

More than any other American of his age, Abraham Lincoln recognized the implications of the expanding concept of total conflict. Whatever the depth of the American predicament, it was obvious to him that the nation could not escape indefinitely the obligation to re-solve it. In June, 1858, he reminded his Springfield audi-ence that the conflict over slavery had increased steadily. Nor would it cease, he warned, "until a *crisis* shall have been reached and passed. 'A house divided against itself cannot stand.' I believe this government cannot endure, permanently *half slave* and *half free*. I do not expect the Union to be dissolved—I do not expect the house to fall —but I do expect it will cease to be divided. It will be-come *all* one thing, or *all* the other." Unless slavery were limited and controlled by Federal action, Lincoln be-lieved, it would triumph totally. Defending his House Divided speech, Lincoln phrased his program for disposing of the slavery question: "I have declared a thousand times, and now repeat that, in my opinion, neither the General Government, nor any other power outside of the slave states, can constitutionally or rightfully interfere with slaves or slavery where it already exists. I believe that whenever the effort to spread slavery into the New Ter-ritories, by whatever means, and into the free States them-selves, by Supreme Court decision, shall be fairly headed off, the institution will then be in course of ultimate extinction. . . ."

Lincoln dramatized the power struggle in terms that

Americans could understand. Continued coexistence between freedom and slavery was precarious, because one must triumph over the other. Having termed the *status quo* unstable and dangerous, Lincoln permitted the nation only two alternatives. Either the South would evolve peacefully toward freedom or the country would suffer violence. But Lincoln, like many of his antislavery colleagues, discovered in the limited program of free soilism the means to resolve the conflict peacefully on Northern terms. If Kansas remained free, he insisted, the entire slave structure would crumble. This doctrine permitted him to speak the language of moderation and promise simultaneously the ultimate triumph of Northern principles. Whatever Lincoln's peaceful intent in achieving such a grand objective, freedom's victory still required no less than a Constitutional amendment or the unconditional surrender of the slaveholders to the antislavery demands of the North. It seemed clear in the late fifties that such a capitulation would result only from some deep conviction in the South that slavery had become a material liability, and as late as 1860 that conviction was nowhere apparent. For most Southerners slavery was not a moral issue at all. Possessing no realistic formula for achieving the peaceful elimination of slavery against the South's determination to maintain it, neither Lincoln nor any other antislavery politician of the North could present to the nation any genuine alternative but civil war to indefinite coexistence with slavery.

IV

What distinguished the political moderates of the North from the antislavery politicians during the fifties was less their attitude toward slavery than their recognition of the North's limited power to establish freedom in the South. That they refused to speak the language of liberty was no evidence that they lacked compassion for the slave. Rather it reflected their conviction that sectional agitation would create illusions of power and fear that had no relation to reality. Antislavery campaigning, they saw, would not terminate in freedom, but in war. They understood better than the extremists that it was beyond the power of the North to free the slaves without tearing the nation apart physically. For them the price was too high. They would tolerate what they could not destroy.

Northern conservatives, in opposing slavery, measured policy by the sole criterion of achievability. For that reason they distinguished clearly between the issues of universal freedom and freedom for the territories, for the latter alone lay within the jurisdiction of governmental action. No American preserved the distinction between the ideal and the real more precisely than did Henry Clay. During the Texas debates he warned Giddings that "the power over the Institution of Slavery in the Slave States is vested exclusively in them." On the other hand, said Clay, "I never can and never will vote, and no earthly power will ever make me vote, to spread slavery over territory where it does not already exist."

It is doubtful if any Northern editor or politician between 1845 and 1860 favored the expansion of slavery; many preferred simply to limit the institution, not through appeals to principle, but through the day-to-day formulation of actual policy. "I do not know of any tribunal on earth that can decide the question of the morality of

slavery or any other institution," admitted Douglas in
September, 1859. "I deal with slavery as a political question involving questions of public policy. I deal with
slavery under the Constitution, and that is all I have to
do with it. . . ." For Douglas the North's security lay
in its superior numbers, not in its superior morality.

In conceding principle, Northern moderates never
conceded any element of their political power. They
denied the existence of an aggressive slavocracy, for they
recognized the essential fact that no Southern element,
representing a minority section badly divided within
itself on all questions of national policy, could have its
way in the Federal Government without powerful Northern support. The annexation of Texas, the passage of the
Walker Tariff of 1846, and the Mexican War were no
evidence of a Southern conspiracy. They were the achieve-
ments of the national Democratic Party, supported as
much by Northern as by Southern party leaders. What
made the South troublesome to Northern economic interests was its philosophical domination by agriculture, not
slavery. If the South wielded major influence in national
life, it was because many Northern politicians responded
to the interests of Northern agriculture, not the interests
of Northern industry. For moderates, whether Whig or
Democratic, the fundamental struggle in the nation was
not between freedom and slavery, but between agriculture
and industry.

Conservatives, quite convinced that any sectional
political movement powerful enough to injure their organizations would also imperil the Union, attempted to
defend the old parties from the corroding effect of the
slavery issue. The Democratic platform of 1844, for exam-

ple, resolved that Congress had no power to control the domestic institutions of the several states. It charged that all efforts to interfere with slavery in the South "are calculated to lead to the most alarming and dangerous consequences, and . . . have an inevitable tendency to diminish the happiness of the people and endanger the stability and permanency of the Union, and ought not to be countenanced by any friend to our political Institutions." This plea for tolerance of slavery was repeated in the Democratic platforms of 1848, 1852, and 1856.

If Northern conservatives spoke the language of coexistence, they wielded sufficient political power to assure their Southern Whig and Democratic colleagues that slavery would not expand. For the Democrats in 1848 and thereafter, the principle of popular sovereignty transferred the issue of slavery expansion to the territories where Northern majorities would rule. The Whigs, promising that their popular candidate of 1848, General Zachary Taylor, would not veto the Wilmot Proviso, placed the issue squarely before Congress where other Northern majorities would control. So obvious was the Northern power and determination to limit slavery to the South that the vast majority of Southerners simply conceded defeat on the issue. The Compromise of 1850 was eminently satisfactory to conservative politicians because it wrote the concept of limited Southern power into law.

Old-line Whigs and Democrats had tied their political fortunes to the established party organizations just as antislavery politicians gambled on the triumph of the third-party movement in the North. With the demise of either the Whig or Democratic Party, thousands of politicians would be cast adrift on the political sea, without an organization or hope of success. Since a Northern party, whatever its political strength, could achieve little more in the actual frustration of Southern purpose than the established parties, conservative politicians viewed the third-party movement as a purely political maneuver to substitute one set of party organizations for another. They regarded the concept of total conflict, the denial that coexistence was possible, as an effort of Northern politicians to manufacture and exploit sectional fears for political ends.

For Whig and Democratic leaders the Republican Party really had no legitimate reason to exist. As a free-soil party it was superfluous. As an agency for attacking the institutions of the South it was dangerous. In either case, it was rendering no service to the Republic. Richard W. Thompson, the Terre Haute, Indiana, Whig, accused the antislavery politicians of having no purpose other than that of achieving power. "They have no ideas about slavery and office," he wrote in 1855. "If they can only exterminate slavery and all the national men of the North, then they'll have *all the offices.* That is the summit of their ambition."

What disturbed Northern Democrats especially was the fact that free soilism could have political mileage only to the extent that Republicans convinced the North that popular sovereignty would encourage rather than prevent the expansion of slavery in the territories. In attacking a moderate program, one anchored to Northern majorities, as one that served only the interests of the South, Republican spokesmen were rendering further compromise between the two sections almost impossible. In accusing the Republican Party of needlessly threatening the Union through such devices, the Indianapolis *Locomotive* concluded resignedly in May, 1856: "It is singular that men will risk the destruction of their country for the success of party—but it is even so." Similarly Douglas decried Republican efforts to exploit the issue of slavery expansion when actually the danger of its occurring did not exist. "Why should we," he declared at Alton in October, 1858, "allow a sectional party to agitate this country, to array the North against the South, and convert us into enemies instead of friends, merely that a few ambitious men may ride into power on a sectional hobby?"

At Quincy that same month, Douglas, in accusing Lincoln of employing moral questions to avoid the necessity of facing the genuine political issues before the nation, summarized the entire conservative argument on slavery. Said Douglas:

He [Lincoln] tells you that I will not argue the question whether slavery is right or wrong. I tell you why I will not do it. I hold that under the Constitution of the United States, each state of this Union has a right to do as it pleases on the subject of slavery. . . . Hence I do not choose to occupy the time allotted to me in discussing a question that we have no right to act upon. I thought that you desired to hear us upon those questions coming within our constitutional power of action. Lincoln will not discuss these. What one question has he discussed that comes within the power or calls for the action or interference of an United States Senator? He is going to discuss the rightfulness of slavery when Congress cannot act upon it either way. He wishes to discuss the merits of the Dred Scott decision when under the Constitution, a Senator has no right to interfere with the decision of judicial tribunals. He wants your exclusive attention to two questions that he has no power to act upon; to two questions that he could not vote upon if he was in Congress, to two questions that are not practical, in order to conceal your attention from other questions which he might be required to vote upon should he ever become a member of Congress. . . .

There was logic in Douglas' position. By 1859 his attack on the Kansas Lecompton Constitution and the complete rejection of the resubmitted document by the people of Kansas convinced many Northerners that Douglas and his doctrine of popular sovereignty were as much a defense against slavery expansion as was the Wilmot Proviso. State Republican platforms, especially in the Midwest, began to ignore the question of Congressional prohibition. One Indiana convention declared that the principle of popular sovereignty was "as old as our government, and that the Republican party now, as ever, is ready to stand and abide by it." In speech after speech Ohio's popular, if reluctant, Republican leader, Thomas Corwin, agreed with Douglas that the people of Kansas alone had the right to determine the nature of their state institutions. As the New York *Times* pointed out, whatever party won in 1860, the issue of slavery in the territories was settled. And the Louisville *Journal* added in February, 1860, that since Kansas was free the Republican Party had no reason for further existence.

What confused the Republican position on slavery even further was the inclination of its leaders to add to the party's program a variety of objectives which ranged from free homesteads to protective tariffs and a transcontinental railroad. But despite the evidence of growing party conservatism, powerful elements within the Republican organization made it clear that their party was fundamentally disinterested in Douglas' concept of coexistence. The uncompromising antislavery forces reminded the politicians that vigorous anti-Southernism was still the most direct and easily traveled road to political power. Practical Republicans understood that any general movement within the party to call off the crusade for universal freedom would result in the creation of a new Northern party that would not be so remiss. When Republican Congressman William Kellogg of Illinois suggested a settlement in the territories on a return to the Missouri Compromise line (the abrogation of which had led to the formation of the Republican Party), his comparative isolation indicated to what extent the continued existence of the party necessitated more than mere freedom for Kansas.

Moreover, the violent Republican attacks on Douglas, required by the political need of wearing down the Northern Democracy, made the Republican Party appear even more radical than it was. Since Douglas opposed the expansion of slavery and thousands of Republicans admitted it, the official Republican charges that Douglas' views were unacceptable to the nonslavery North permitted no conclusion but that the Republican Party was engaged in a continuing war against the South's institutions. Indeed, conservative members of the Northern press wondered why Douglas, in the interest of national unity, did not join the Republican free soilers in an effort to demonstrate to the South that even the vast majority of Republicans believed fundamentally in continued coexistence. But Douglas, as a Democratic politician, was as devoted to the perpetuation of his party organization as his Republican opponents were dedicated to its destruction.

V

Unfortunately, after the Dred Scott decision, many influential Southerners refused to accept coexistence any longer even on Douglas' terms. Until 1857 the Southern rationale, first created by John C. Calhoun in February, 1847, which denied Congress the right to limit slavery in the territories and consigned the final decision to a state constitution, remained an abstraction, totally meaningless as a program for extending slavery amid the facts of westward expansion. For that reason it had made little progress toward general acceptance even in the South. The Nashville convention of June, 1850, offered a settlement to the Pacific along the Missouri Compromise line. Most Southerners were convinced that slavery would not cross that line, and they had no interest in a fight over principles alone. Their lack of attention to the Kansas-Nebraska Bill revealed again their conviction that principles were unimportant when they collided with the North's superior numbers.

Chief Justice Roger B. Taney's argument in the Dred Scott case confronted the South with its last fateful decision. That section could anchor its future security either to the legality of its principles or to the continuance of the national Democratic Party. It could not do both. Democratic unity demanded that Calhoun's claims remain buried out of sight. But the Dred Scott decision gave them a new twist and a new significance by making them the law of the land. This eased the task of Southern extremists, who placed principles above party, to inflame and agitate the Southern mind into believing that the future of Southern society rested on the hopeless question of slavery expansion. From Taney's decision onward, the national Democratic leadership would struggle for party harmony against insurmountable odds.

Douglas' Freeport Doctrine of 1858 threatened what remained of national cohesion as embodied in the national Democratic organization, for he attributed to popular sovereignty the power to nullify the Dred Scott decision. Southern extremists refused to concede to the North's superior numbers. Relying on the principle of equality in the territories, they demanded that the Federal Government underwrite the Dred Scott decision by voting troops to protect any slave minority in the territories. Convinced as well that Kansas was overwhelmingly antislavery, they were determined that Kansas remain outside the Union, preferably forever.

During 1859 those Southerners who argued for principle appeared to be in the ascendancy, although the North challenged the slave system only in the territories where principles were meaningless. How Kansas could bring victory or defeat to the South was not clear. But to meet the Northern challenge in the territories without equivocation, Southern Democratic leaders were determined not only to dispose of Douglas and his views on popular sovereignty, but also to expose the South's deeper struggle with the Republican Party. Whether its unfinished program lay in Whiggery or liberation, that party appeared a vital threat to the interests of the South.

In November, 1859, the Richmond *Enquirer* demanded that the delegates to the forthcoming Demo-

cratic convention at Charleston draw "a line of demarca-
tion—broad and distinct, in platform and candidate, from
Black Republicanism." The Memphis *Avalanche* similarly
asked that the convention recognize that the Republican
Party was the real enemy of the South. "If the Dred Scott
decision is to be trampled in the dust, and the sacred
right of property . . . repudiated," ran one editorial of
October, 1859, "for heaven's sake let the infamous outrage be committed in the name of Black Republicanism
instead of Democracy." Southern politicians, in their
fundamental decision to demand more of the North than
a united Democratic Party would secure for them, had at
last joined the antislavery politicians in the tragic dilemma of expecting the triumph of abstract principles
which were totally unachievable within the limits of the
American democratic structure. By 1859 many Southerners admitted openly their preference for Southern independence to any concession of sectional rights which
might endanger the profits of cotton, tobacco, and slavery.

By 1860 American politics had reached the dead end
predicted for it by the very nature of the slavery issue.
Dominant political elements of both the North and the
South demanded of the nation what they could achieve
only in defiance of the Constitution. But for the American
people there was no escape from the eternal predicament
to which the politicians had consigned them. Northern
campaigning assured the country that it could never retreat again from the moral implications of slavery. Lincoln chided the South for its intolerance of the Republican Party. Nothing that the South could do, other than
freeing its slaves, would quiet the Northern conscience.
Antislavery sentiment, he reminded the South, commanded

a million and a half votes. But had that number been twice as large, the question of slavery's future would have been no nearer solution.

Whether those who wielded political power could resolve the slavery issue or not, they could not turn from it without destroying the political machines they had created. Neither could they move forward, for there was no answer in American politics to the moral problems which they had singled out for agitation and exploitation. What the antislavery forces of the North demanded for the Republic could not even be achieved through violence unless the forceful liberation of the slaves were legalized through Constitutional amendment. Yet politicians whose successful employment of the slavery issue had placed them in the political ascendancy were prepared to drive their emotional advantages even further in 1860. Beyond their campaigning there could be only continued vituperation, continued magnification of moral sentiment that could never be satisfied, continued governmental inaction until the nation would relieve itself of its moral and political dilemma through the only means remaining—civil war.

Well could the thoughtful editor of the New York *Times* observe in September, 1859: "It is time that we should begin to see whither the country is to drift in the approaching national canvass. . . ."

DON E. FEHRENBACHER

II

The Republican Decision at Chicago

Whatever disagreement there may be about the underlying causes of the Civil War, it is clear that the conflict
was precipitated in 1860-61 by a series of momentous
decisions which began with the election of a Republican
president. True, the causal connection between these
decisions cannot be regarded as one of necessity. Secession
followed closely upon Abraham Lincoln's victory, but
reasonable alternatives presented themselves to Southern
leaders, the most obvious one being to wait for an overt
act of Republican aggression before taking such a drastic
step. The fact that eight of the slaveholding states did
choose to temporize leads one to doubt that the action
of the other seven was utterly compulsive. At the same
time, the danger of disunion was unquestionably older
than the Republican Party and would not have been
swept away by a different verdict at the polls in 1860.
Some event other than the election of Lincoln could
have brought on the final crisis, for there were many

aspects of the discord between North and South, and the idea of secession had been thoroughly domesticated in the Southern mind.

Nevertheless, as it happened, the Republican victory in 1860 proved to be that particular link between causes and effects which is sometimes called the "occasion." Without it, things would have been different, perhaps even vastly different, depending upon how delicate the balance really was between violence and accommodation. As for Lincoln, the fact that he was the choice of his party probably had no significant influence upon the Southern decision to secede. Black Republicans all looked alike to the Cotton Kingdom. But in the determination of how secession should be answered, the character of the new president became extremely important, and it made a difference that Lincoln, instead of the more protean William H. Seward, had won the nomination at Chicago. Therefore, to discover why the Civil War started when it did and in the way that it did, it is necessary to inquire how the Republican Party came to be what it was in 1860; namely, a political organization conservative enough to win a presidential election, yet provocative enough to set off a major rebellion. And much of the essence of early Republicanism is revealed in the elevation of Abraham Lincoln to party leadership.

Robust at birth and swift to achieve power, the Republican Party has flourished for so long as one component of a stable two-party system that Americans often forget the precarious uncertainty of its first years and look upon it as a favored child of destiny. It is true that Republicanism gave expression to certain powerful forces and aspirations in American life which were probably irrepressible. The demands of an emerging industrial capitalism and an expanding frontier, the urgency of humanitarian reform, presumably could not have been stifled by any conceivable means. Yet the precise form which this expression took, as well as the speed and amplitude of its success, resulted in no small part from accident, luck, and free decision.

For one thing, the Republican Party made its appearance at a time of extraordinary political turmoil—a condition directly attributable to the furious controversy over the Kansas-Nebraska Bill, but also having deeper roots. Apart from the disruptive effects of sectional discord upon institutional forms, instability and fragmentation had always been as much the rule as the exception in American politics. The so-called "presidential synthesis" of our history exaggerates the substantialness of national parties before the Civil War and obscures the decentralized, diverse, and mutable character of political association at the state and local level. There, the party insurgent, the bolted convention, the splinter group, the improvised coalition, and the call for a new party were virtually routine aspects of the political process. One of the reasons, for instance, why a Republican organization took shape so quickly in Wisconsin during 1854 was that there had been a kind of dress rehearsal the year before in the form of a short-lived "People's Party." These strong centrifugal tendencies in the political heritage and environment of the 1850's were highly conducive to the emergence of new combinations like the Republican Party, but prejudicial to their subsequent growth and integration. Why Republicanism was born is perhaps a less important question than how it survived.

Don E. Fehrenbacher

Despite the suddenness with which the Republican Party entered upon the scene in 1854, it was in some degree the culmination of a trend toward political sectionalism which had already produced the free-soil movement of 1848. The causes of this trend have long been a subject of dispute among historians. Opposition to slavery, certainly the most conspicuous factor, once received almost exclusive attention. But then a reaction set in, and it became the scholarly fashion to emphasize economic motives. The agrarian South, according to Charles A. Beard and others, was under attack primarily because it stood in the way of tariff protection, internal improvements, and all the other needs of a new, industrial America. The Republican Party thus served as the political agency of an economic revolution which eventually freed capitalism from the restraints imposed upon it by the slave power.

One variant of the Beard thesis stressed the clash of the two labor systems, and particularly their competition for Western lands. "The Republican party was not an anti-slavery party," wrote John R. Commons. "It was a homestead party. . . . Only because slavery could not live on one-hundred-and-sixty-acre farms did the Republican party come into conflict with slavery." Wilfred E. Binkley, in his well-known history of American political parties, subscribed wholeheartedly to the Commons view, declaring that the slavery issue was "merely incidental" to the Republicans' fundamental purpose of "ensuring the West to free laborers and farmers." Still another interpretation is summarized by Reinhard H. Luthin when he says that the "cohesive force" within the new Republican Party was not anti-Southern sentiment at all, but hostility to the Democrats—in other words, the "eagerness of the 'outs' to get 'in.' " A large part of the Republican leadership, Luthin maintains, was "amazingly indifferent" to the problem of slavery, but aware of its emotional value as a "vote-getting issue." In this line of reasoning, slavery and economic questions together become merely the manipulative features of a fierce struggle for political power.

Such attempts to isolate the quintessence of Republicanism bring to mind the story of the blind men trying to describe an elephant, each with his hand upon a different part of the creature's body. The burden of proof rests, however, on those who deny what seems obvious— that opposition to slavery constituted the emotional core and unifying principle of the early Republican Party. Indifference there undoubtedly was, and naked opportunism too, but if these attitudes were typically Republican, then a veritable mountain of historical evidence is false, and hypocrisy had become a dominant American trait in the 1850's. As for economic influences, they were capable of reinforcing the Republican movement, but not of initiating or integrating it. The basic flaw in the Beard approach is that it judged the Republican Party by what it became after the Civil War, and thus erroneously converted consequences into original intentions. Only the steady growth of a Northern consensus on the moral unacceptability of slavery explains either the rise of Republicanism or its brilliant success in contrast with the disintegration of Whiggery, the failure of Know-Nothingism, and the disruption of the Democracy.

The core of a thing is by no means the whole of it,

however, and it must be recognized that the word "slavery" acquired many connotative meanings, that a complex set of collateral values, interests, and ambitions attached themselves to the antislavery principle. As a result, various other issues were wrenched from their natural contexts and fused with the problem of Negro servitude. Slavery thus became as much a symbolic as a concrete factor in the sectional conflict, but this does not mean that the attack upon the institution itself was synthetic or "incidental." Indeed, the tendency of nearly all public controversy to fall into alignment with the slavery question bespeaks the power with which that question gripped the minds of the American people.

II

The main features of Republicanism were anticipated in the Free Soil Party of 1848, an alliance of insurgent Whigs and Democrats, together with abolitionists, which was dedicated to the exclusion of slavery from the Federal territories. The party platform, significantly, also set forth an economic program embracing river and harbor improvements, free land for settlers, and an adequate revenue tariff. In the presidential election, to be sure, the Free Soilers ran far behind the two major parties and polled less than 15 per cent of the total *Northern* vote. But this figure, which compares so unfavorably with Fremont's 45 per cent in 1856 and Lincoln's 55 per cent in 1860, considerably understates the actual Free Soil strength, for many persons in strong sympathy with the movement were unwilling to throw away their votes upon it. And although the party itself went into rapid decline after the territorial question was temporarily settled in 1850, the free-soil spirit remained a powerful, half-latent force in American politics, ready to erupt at any time through another outlet.

The Kansas-Nebraska Bill of 1854 crystallized anti-slavery feeling once more and at the same time augmented it. Just why this measure should have been so much more devastating in its effect on political structures than the Wilmot Proviso controversy of the 1840's is not easy to explain. One may point, however, to signs of cumulative stress. Grievances, both political and economic, had been piling up, especially in the Northwest, and there was an increasing disposition to regard the "slave power" as the tyrannical source of every affliction and frustration. Furthermore, the constant strain of sectional antagonism had undoubtedly eroded the cohesive strength of the two major parties and brought the Whigs in particular to the verge of disintegration. But the Nebraska matter, while raising the same old question of slavery in the territories, put it in new and explosive terms. The proponents of the Wilmot Proviso had been on the offensive, attempting to bar slavery from all newly conquered land. In resisting the repeal of the Missouri Compromise, however, antislavery forces were fighting a desperate defensive battle to preserve gains long since won for freedom. The impression that freedom had been thrown on the defensive by an aggressive slave power was reinforced by later events like the Dred Scott decision, and it accounts in no small degree for the broader appeal of the antislavery cause after 1854.

The violent popular revulsion in the North against the Kansas-Nebraska Act furnished a basis for the first antislavery party of major proportions, but in the beginning it produced only an extremely loose and tentative coalition. It is true that in some areas a new political organization calling itself "Republican" began to emerge during the summer of 1854. Yet many outspoken critics of the Nebraska policy held aloof at least temporarily from the Republican movement, and a sizable number of them never joined it. For example, ten counties in central Illinois (including Lincoln's own Sangamon) which were anti-Nebraska in 1854 voted Democratic in 1860. The consolidation of seemingly incompatible elements like Whigs and Democrats, nativists and foreigners, radicals and conservatives into a single party proceeded at varying speeds throughout the free states and was not substantially accomplished for several years. Moreover, with just the single bond of anti-Nebraska sentiment uniting its diverse membership, Republicanism could not at first enunciate a comprehensive political program. This explains the narrowness of the national platform drafted in 1856, which concentrated almost exclusively upon the slavery question. It also helps to explain the nomination of John C. Fremont, a colorful celebrity who was conveniently vague in his politics, except on the subject of slavery.

By confining their attention to a single major issue, the early Republicans were able to achieve numerical strength and some degree of solidarity, but this was a fragile basis upon which to build a permanent organization. What would happen to a party with only one stated purpose if events should strip that purpose of its relevance? The Kansas-Nebraska Act itself, for all the indignation that it aroused, did not constitute a durable issue, especially since there was no hope of repealing the measure. Soon, however, the struggle had been transferred to the Western plains. It was the disorder and violence in Kansas which kept the anti-Nebraska coalition alive and helped convert it into a major political party. Yet there remained always the possibility that a sudden and complete pacification of Kansas would deprive Republicanism of its reason for being.

Certain factors in American politics encourage adherence to the two-party system, one of them being the way in which the nation chooses its presidents. By 1855, there were indications that the simple and familiar two-party arrangement might soon be restored, but exactly what would replace the disappearing Whig Party was still far from clear. Republican organizations were strong in some Northern states, weak or half-formed or nonexistent in others. Meanwhile, political nativism was competing for the role of major opposition to the Democracy. Know-Nothingism had become dominant in much of New England; it was powerful enough in New York to win the state election of 1855; and it seemed likely to gain the upper hand in New Jersey and Pennsylvania. Less potent in the Northwest, the Know-Nothings nevertheless held the balance of power in Indiana and Illinois. Furthermore, the movement had the added advantage over Republicanism of appealing to many Southerners, and thus of presenting itself as a national, rather than a sectional, alternative to Democratic misrule. On the other hand, a majority of Northern Know-Nothings were also anti-Nebraskans, and as the turmoil continued in Kansas they became more and more inclined to place slavery ahead of the foreigner on their agenda of public problems. As a result, the American Party had hardly been organized on a national basis before it began to break apart. When the "North Americans" decided to support Fremont instead of Millard Fillmore in 1856, the future of Republicanism seemed secure.

The presidential election of 1856, which returned a Democrat to the White House, had a decisive influence upon subsequent Republican strategy. First, the election established the Republican Party indisputably as the major party of opposition to the Democrats. Although defeated, it had carried eleven of the sixteen free states and was apparently still gathering momentum. Second, the American Party, even though it won only a handful of electoral votes, nevertheless had demonstrated impressive strength. Fillmore, while making his best showing in the Southern border states, polled nearly 400,000 votes in the North and unquestionably hurt Fremont more than he did Buchanan. Third, the election had been decided in the states of the lower North, where Fremont carried only Ohio and Iowa, while losing New Jersey, Pennsylvania, Indiana, and Illinois, together with California. Thus the battle areas for 1860 were clearly defined. In order to elect a president, the Republicans would have to hold all of their gains and, in addition, capture several of the five free states lost to Buchanan, including the almost indispensable Pennsylvania. This meant that they had to convert the bulk of the conservative Whig-Americans who had cast some 200,000 votes for Fillmore in those states. How to woo the Fillmore men, how to win the doubtful states, became subjects of endless discussion among Republican strategists.

One seemingly obvious course was more or less out of the question. Any general appeal to nativist sentiment

would alienate the numerous foreign-born Republicans
and soil the party's cloak of high idealism. However, since
the antislavery foreigners were overwhelmingly Protes-
tant, while the Catholic sons of Ireland tended to remain
loyal Democrats, there was some room for exploitation
of the religious prejudice in Know-Nothingism. The Chicago *Tribune* stated the case with admirable clarity in
1856 when it declared that the Republican Party was
just the place for the man who wanted to "repress the
political tendencies of a false but arrogant church, without ostracizing the foreigner whose political and religious
sympathies [were] as true and ardent as his own." Anti-
Catholicism, although it was never more than one of the
fringe themes of Republicanism, entered into denuncia-
tions of the Dred Scott decision (Taney being a Catholic)
and into attacks upon Douglas, who, having taken a
Catholic wife, was frequently depicted as a potential tool
of the Pope.

The line of action favored by certain Republican
leaders was a remodeling of the party to give it broader
appeal. A little more flexibility on the subject of slavery
would probably bring many Fillmore men, and even
some Democrats, into the fold; a stronger emphasis upon
economic matters would awaken the interest of persons
relatively indifferent to the antislavery crusade. But these
were steps to be taken only after careful deliberation because they might lead to serious internal dissension, or to
the submergence of Republican identity in a barren and
faceless opportunism. Lincoln, for one, was apprehensive
about such strategy, and up to the time of his nomination
not only opposed any retreat on the slavery issue but also
advised against inserting a tariff plank in the platform.

In the end, the election of 1856 had its most significant effect upon Republican thinking when it suggested the kind of presidential candidate needed in 1860. For as the months went by, there was a growing conviction in many quarters that the nominee must be especially attractive to conservative Whig-Americans and able to run well in the doubtful states of the lower North.

III

Bleeding Kansas had been the main issue of the campaign, its importance enhanced by the civil war there which reached its climax in the late summer of 1856. But then, with the appointment of a new governor, some degree of peace was restored in the territory, and it appeared that the Republicans might at last be running out of battles to fight. Not for long, however. During the first year of the Buchanan administration, one event after another opened up new areas of controversy. "Seldom if ever," wrote Albert J. Beveridge, "has a political party been so favored by fortune as were the Republicans during 1857."

First came the Dred Scott decision, a judicial assault upon the cardinal principle of Republicanism which provoked a storm of protest from the antislavery forces and strengthened their determination to rescue the Federal Government from its Southern masters. Next, the worst financial panic in twenty years struck the country, bringing bankruptcies, unemployment, and the general gloom of hard times that always militates against the party in power. The depression, by increasing public discontent with Democratic policies on the tariff, homesteads, and internal improvements, cleared the way for the broader

economic program introduced into the Republican platform of 1860. Still another boon to the Republicans was
the military expedition of 1857-58 against the Mormons
in Utah. Hastily planned and humiliating in some of its
consequences, this venture damaged the administration's
prestige, made a mockery of popular sovereignty, and
dramatized the urgent need for a transcontinental railroad. Then, on top of these developments, the Kansas
question flamed up again when the Lecompton Constitution, weighted in favor of slavery, was submitted to
Congress.

Buchanan's attempt to secure the admission of Kansas as a slave state under the Lecompton instrument caused
a popular outburst in the North not unlike that of 1854,
and once again the political situation became exceedingly
confused and fluid. The most spectacular aspect of the
Lecompton affair was Douglas' bold revolt against the
administration and the resulting split in the Democratic
Party. But the controversy had some unsettling effects
upon the Republicans too, even though they stood to
profit immensely from it. By early 1858, in fact, the party
was approaching a major crossroads in its short history,
and there was considerable disagreement over the direction next to be taken.

The anti-Lecompton battle in Congress, waged by
a coalition of Republicans, Americans, and Douglas
Democrats, inspired thoughts of a new grand alliance
against the slave power. Douglas himself was so open and
enthusiastic in his cooperation with Republican leaders
that a number of them became optimistic about the possibility of a merger. That erratic genius of the newspaper world, Horace Greeley, showered praise upon the

Little Giant and urged that Republicans join in re-electing him to the Senate. Similar views issued from other party journals in the East, including the New York *Times,* Thurlow Weed's Albany *Evening Journal,* and the Springfield (Massachusetts) *Republican,* which declared: "So powerful an instrumentality as Mr. Douglas should not, must not be paralyzed at the very moment when he commences to be of service to the interests of free labor . . . let him not be supplanted by an inferior."

Along with this new-found Republican respect for Douglas went added tolerance for his "great principle." The progress of events in Kansas seemed to indicate that popular sovereignty, when honestly applied, was enough to win the territories for freedom. Seward very nearly conceded as much on the Senate floor. It appeared that the principle of the Wilmot Proviso was losing some of its relevance, that the final struggle would be between those who demanded and those who opposed Federal protection of slavery in the territories. If so, the anti-Lecompton coalition, with its Sewards and Douglases, might well become permanent, replacing or transforming the Republican organization.

Greeley, who loved to play the role of political strategist, saw more than one advantage accruing from the policy that he recommended. His extravagant praise of Douglas was intended to strengthen the ties between Republicans and anti-Lecompton Democrats while widening the breach in the Democratic Party. In addition, Greeley wanted to gather in the Whig-Americans, and he proposed to quiet their fears of Republican radicalism with a display of generosity toward everyone who had opposed the Lecompton Constitution. Douglas, returned in triumph to the Senate, would symbolize the new, conservative phase of the antislavery effort.

These half-developed plans to build a more inclusive opposition party, whatever their chance of success might otherwise have been, ran into angry and adamant resistance from a pivotal group. The Republicans of Illinois, spurning the suggestion that they support Douglas, and denouncing the presumptuous interference of "outsiders," proclaimed their determination to elect no man but Abraham Lincoln. Any lingering uncertainty was removed in an unprecedented manner on June 16, 1858, when the Republican state convention boisterously approved a resolution designating Lincoln as its "first and only" choice for senator. The memorable contest between Lincoln and Douglas then followed, and the latter's brief flirtation with Republicanism came to an end. Meanwhile, Greeley had already peevishly conceded the right of Illinois Republicans to choose their own candidate. "I am weary of trying to pound any reason into their heads," he complained to a friend. But the New York editor's general viewpoint remained unchanged, and it was soon reflected in his support of Edward Bates, conservative Missouri Whig, for the Republican presidential nomination.

It is therefore possible that events in Illinois prevented the emergence of a new political coalition which, because of its conservatism, might have blunted the secession movement and guided the nation past the danger of civil war. In the circumstances, however, the decision of the Illinois Republicans was almost inevitable. Their animosity toward Douglas was too deep and personal to be set aside at anyone's bidding. "Dragooning the republicans of this State into the support of Douglas . . . is an abomination too hateful even for these times of general corruption and profligacy," one man exclaimed. "I am not willing," said another, "that we . . . who have received so much abuse at his hands should now turn round and endorse his traitorous cause by giving him the highest office in our hands." The Chicago *Tribune* protested that "if the Republicans of Illinois should . . . re-elect Mr. Douglas, their party would be so disintegrated that the State would be lost to freedom in 1860." But it was Lincoln, as usual, who contributed the most trenchant comment. "My judgment is," he wrote, "that we must never sell old friends to buy old enemies."

Lincoln's views were shaped only in part by personal ambition, for he was utterly convinced that collaboration with Douglas would destroy the Republican Party and with it all hope of achieving an early settlement of the slavery issue. The question, he told Lyman Trumbull shortly after the debates of 1858, was whether the Republican organization would "maintain its identity, or be broken up to form the tail of Douglas' new kite." There was consequently a practical purpose as well as deep conviction in his emphasis upon the moral aspect of the slavery problem, and in his insistence that Kansas was "neither the whole nor a tithe of the real question." That purpose was to differentiate sharply between the basic assumptions and ultimate objectives of Republicanism on the one hand and of Douglasism on the other.

The Republicans, according to Lincoln, believed that slavery was wrong and proposed to treat it as a wrong within the limits of the Constitution, while hoping for its eventual extinction by some peaceful means. Douglas, having little moral objection to the institution, was willing to let it compete as an equal with freedom and saw no reason why the nation should not survive forever, half slave and half free. But in the end, Lincoln maintained, one principle or the other must conquer. A house divided against itself could not stand. And Douglas, whether intentionally or not, Lincoln believed, was serving as "miner and sapper" for the proslavery forces, because his doctrine of calculated indifference was helping to prepare the public mind for the nationalization of slavery.

Thus Lincoln stood opposed to any lowering of the Republican platform for the purpose of accommodating Northern conservatives. Instead, he would accentuate the gulf between those who believed and those who did not believe that slavery was wrong, and then try to persuade all members of the first group that they belonged in the Republican ranks.

Yet if Lincoln's inflexibility on the territorial question was motivated in some degree by an assiduous concern for the welfare of his party, it also stemmed from conviction, and particularly from his recognition of the question's symbolic importance. To him, the restriction of slavery was not only a practical objective in itself, but an instrument for settling a far more fundamental issue— the very moral status of slavery in a nation dedicated to human liberty. "Never forget," he told a Chicago audience in 1859, "that we have before us this whole matter of the right or wrong of slavery in this Union, though the immediate question is as to its spreading out into new Territories and States." For Lincoln, in other words, slavery restriction was necessary most of all as a commitment to freedom, as an orientation toward that distant goal which he had labeled "ultimate extinction."

IV

The year 1860 found the youthful Republican Party well organized and resolute, but still comparatively plastic, still awaiting the final molding of its character. Election victories in 1858 and 1859, especially those in Pennsylvania, and the continuing division of the Democrats, inspired a general feeling of optimism. On the other hand, the John Brown raid threw Republican leaders temporarily on the defensive, and the preliminary organization of the Constitutional Union Party in February darkened prospects of absorbing the Whig-Americans. Everywhere the need was felt to present Republicanism as safely conservative, worthy to exercise power. Lincoln's Cooper Union address of February 27, while yielding nothing in the matter of principle, was soberly phrased, devoid of the more provocative themes in his House Divided speech, and designed to demonstrate historically that the Republicans were the true intellectual heirs of the Founding Fathers. Seward, delivering a major speech on the Senate floor two days later, was almost frantically conservative in his plea for reconciliation between what he euphemistically termed the "capital" states of the South and the "labor" states of the North. Some antislavery radicals entered bitter protests against any retreat from aggressive Republicanism, but many others were willing to make at least limited concessions in order to accomplish the overthrow of the slave power. As the date of their national convention approached, Republicans became increasingly nervous about the decisions they must make. The question debated over and over was whether the party had enough strength to elect its most representative leader or needed to seek out its most available one. And so at Chicago in the third week of May, the Republican Party, pulled this way and that by men, events, and the calculations of strategy, at last achieved some measure of self-definition.

The Republican platform of 1860 was drafted by a subcommittee comprised primarily of Westerners, although a Pennsylvanian acted as chairman. In general, historians have pronounced its slavery planks "conservative" in comparison with those of 1856. This view, while not without some basis in fact, is often fortified by a misreading of the document.

The subcommittee did delete the offensive reference to "those twin relics of barbarism—polygamy and slavery," and it added a section which in effect condemned the John Brown raid. Furthermore, the cardinal principle of Republicanism was restated in more flexible terms. Instead of insisting upon "positive legislation" prohibiting slavery in every territory, the party promised to enact such legislation whenever it should become "necessary." This might appear to be a partial acceptance of Douglas' doctrine of popular sovereignty, but not so. Later passages specifically denied the power of a territorial legislature to "give legal existence to slavery" and denounced popular sovereignty as a "deception and fraud." The net effect was to offer a territory the choice of excluding slavery itself or having it done by Congress. Republicans still proposed to skin their cat, but now acknowledged two ways of doing it.

Other sections of the platform censured illegal trade

in African slaves, called for the immediate admission of Kansas, and repudiated the Dred Scott decision without actually naming it. In addition, threats of disunion were sharply denounced as "an avowal of contemplated treason," which it was "the imperative duty of an indignant people sternly to rebuke and forever silence." On the whole, and in spite of numerous assertions to the contrary, the platform of 1860 appears to have been more comprehensive and scarcely less forceful than that of 1856 in its treatment of slavery and related issues.

Of the last five planks in the platform, one took a forthright antinativist stand against changes in naturalization laws and the abridgment of citizenship rights "hitherto accorded to immigrants from foreign lands." The others, endorsing a Pacific railroad, river and harbor improvements, a homestead law, and some degree of tariff protection, constituted the economic portion of the Republican program. The first two of these four items were carried over from 1856; the tariff and homestead sections were new, although both subjects had been dealt with in the Free Soil platform of 1848. All four represented concessions to specific sectional and economic interests, but the Pacific railroad was more or less noncontroversial, since both wings of the Democracy were also pledged to its construction. The other three amounted to flank attacks upon the Southern position, and the homestead proposal in particular may be regarded as the Northern answer to slavery expansion. The tariff plank, a matter of peripheral interest except to Pennsylvania and New Jersey, was mild enough to disarm all but the most extreme opponents of protection.

It is sometimes said that the economic spirit of

Whiggery triumphed in the Republican platform of 1860, but unless one defines Whiggery in terms so broad that they become almost meaningless, this interpretation has only a limited validity and ignores the dynamics of history. The Whigs were certainly identified with protective tariffs and internal improvements, but the latter had increasingly become a sectional rather than a partisan issue, and the tariff in 1860 was more important to Pennsylvania Democrats than to comparatively indifferent Whigs in other states. Moreover, the vital homestead plank was definitely not out of the Whig tradition. Insofar as Republicanism contemplated somewhat more governmental intervention in the economic life of the nation, it may perhaps be loosely associated with the spirit of Henry Clay, but the platform of 1860, like the party itself, was actually an amalgam of many things, including strong elements of Jacksonianism as well as Whiggery.

Any platform is but an imperfect reflection of a party's true character because it serves both as an instrument for obtaining power and a statement of how that power will be used. Thus the Republican platform of 1860 no doubt understates the party's hostility to slavery and probably overstates the amount of general interest in tariff revision. To the limited extent that it serves as a reliable basis for judgment, the document reveals a party concerned primarily with slavery and the slaveholder's extraordinary influence in national politics, secondarily with the exploitation of the great West for the benefit of free labor, and only in a rudimentary way with the promotion of industrial capitalism.

On the convention floor, one major flurry of excitement over the platform occurred when old Joshua Giddings demanded the reinsertion of a quotation from the Declaration of Independence which had appeared in the 1856 document. What followed was not really a test between radicals and conservatives, but rather a debate over how much rhetorical padding should be included in a statement of party principles. After some glowing oratory, the Giddings viewpoint was sustained, and the amended platform then received a unanimous and enthusiastic vote of approval. By now, it was six o'clock in the evening of May 17, the second day of the convention, and the delegates, after some hesitation, chose to adjourn until the next morning instead of proceeding immediately to the nomination of a presidential candidate. This proved to be a crucial decision because it gave the miscellaneous opponents of Seward extra time in which to negotiate with one another.

V

What happened in the Wigwam the next day was a drama in two parts: the rejection of Seward and the nomination of Lincoln. Seward's name had dominated preconvention discussion. A tested veteran of many battles against slavery and a political leader of acknowledged skill, he was the "Mr. Republican" of his era and the logical choice for the presidential nomination. Of course he had acquired numerous enemies in his rise to pre-eminence, but in the end his fate was sealed by a pivotal group of delegates who, without pronounced personal animus, concluded that he would be a dangerously vulnerable candidate. A reputation for radicalism, not entirely deserved, was the first count against the New York Senator. At heart a man of moderate temperament and considerable flexibility, he could not escape the consequences of his phrase-making talent and was remembered best as the prophet of "higher law" and "irrepressible conflict." Equally important, although sometimes less emphasized, Seward's open record of opposition to Know-Nothingism and his long feud with the Fillmore wing of New York Whiggery promised to alienate much of the desperately needed American vote. And at the same time, his close association with Thurlow Weed repelled many party idealists who regarded machine politics as a synonym for corruption. The conduct of the large New York contingent which came to vote and shout for Seward at Chicago deepened the suspicion that his supporters were not altogether respectable. "They can drink as much whiskey," wrote Murat Halstead, "swear as loud and long, sing as bad songs, and 'get up and howl' as ferociously as any crowd of Democrats you ever heard, or heard of."

So the cry was raised that the nomination of Seward would spell defeat, that he could not carry the doubtful states of the lower North. Among the prominent members of this chorus, significantly, were the gubernatorial candidates for Pennsylvania and Indiana. Worried talk about "availability" had been stimulated by Democratic gains in certain New England spring elections and, more recently, by the entry of John Bell and Edward Everett in the presidential race as nominees of the newly organized Constitutional Union Party. As for the spectacular events at Charleston early in May, their total effect was not entirely clear. In itself, the disruption of the opposition brightened Republican prospects and therefore strengthened the case for Seward. But the expected nomination of Douglas by Northern Democrats when they reassembled at Baltimore would bring a powerful figure, freed of association with the slaveholders, into competition for the moderate vote in the free states. With Seward running against the Little Giant, it was argued, the contest might well end in the House of Representatives, where a Republican victory seemed most unlikely.

The opposition to Seward gathered strength during the first two days of the Republican convention, and yet it showed little sign of uniting upon a single candidate. Just before midnight on May 17, a disconsolate Greeley, still campaigning for Bates, sent a telegram to his New York *Tribune* predicting that Seward would be nominated. Even as he did so, however, a discernible trend toward Lincoln was beginning to emerge from the confusion. The skillful work of Lincoln's managers at this juncture undoubtedly contributed much to his success, but it must be emphasized that certain favorable circumstances made their achievement something less than miraculous.

In the first place, Lincoln became Seward's chief rival because the other candidates for that position were exceptionally weak. Salmon P. Chase, the only man approaching Seward's stature as an antislavery leader, was considered more radical than the New Yorker and never had a chance. Some Ohio delegates hoped to drop Chase and start a boom for their uncouth senator, Ben Wade, but the Chase men blocked the scheme. Pennsylvania, with its immense influence, could offer nothing better than Simon Cameron, a political turncoat, reputedly corrupt, and once closely allied with the Know-Nothings. Edward Bates appealed to many conservatives and to strategists like Greeley who wanted to remove the stigma of radicalism and sectionalism from the Republican Party. But he was an elderly, lackluster figure, who had supported Fillmore in 1856 and could hardly be called a Republican at all. His nomination, in addition to offending foreign-born voters and the more dedicated opponents of slavery, would have amounted to a retreat and misrepresentation. The lesser candidates in the field, like William L. Dayton and John McLean, had little hope unless the leaders should falter and the convention become deadlocked.

In addition there was Lincoln, whose qualifications, when scrutinized, proved to be impressive. He seemed moderate in comparison with Seward, primarily because he had been less prominent in the antislavery wars. Personally opposed to nativism, he had never denounced it publicly, and was thus unobjectionable to foreigners and Know-Nothings alike. His greatest handicap, a lack of experience and standing in national politics, had been partially remedied by the series of dramatic encounters with Douglas, which established him in the public mind as the latter's peculiar adversary. His Kentucky birth and frontier background would be campaign assets. As a Westerner and former Whig, he could be trusted to sustain the economic planks in the party platform. And he was the favorite son of Illinois, third behind Pennsylvania and Indiana on the list of critical states. These were the major elements in Lincoln's touted availability. Yet at the same time, and equally important, this product of the Western prairies was firm and forthright in his position on slavery—a thoroughly representative Republican as well as an available one. His nomination would involve no sacrifice of the party's principles, no dilution of its will.

Lincoln's candidacy was built upon a foundation of united support from his own state, the Illinois delegation having been instructed to vote for him as a unit. But it was Indiana that made him a major contender. The Hoosiers, without a candidate of their own, and convinced that Seward could not be elected, gave some thought to Bates but then decided to cast all 26 of their votes for Lincoln on the first ballot. This commitment, a magnificent gain in itself, also helped soften up the Pennsylvania delegates, most of whom now agreed to accept Lincoln as their second choice. The views of Pennsylvania, in turn, exercised a profound influence upon the rest of the convention. Accordingly, when the hour arrived for placing names in nomination, a two-man race had already begun to take shape, with Seward in the lead, but Lincoln possessing the greater momentum.

The first ballot had scarcely begun before it became apparent that Seward was weaker and Lincoln stronger than anyone had expected. Leading off in the roll call, the New England states, with 82 votes at their disposal, gave Seward a disappointing 32, Lincoln a surprising 19. In this, as in each of the succeeding ballots, New England reflected with unusual accuracy the will of the entire convention. The tabulation revealed that Seward had 173½ votes and Lincoln 102, while ten other candidates were scattered far behind. Seward needed only 60 additional votes to win, but he had little room for maneuvering because a conspicuous sectional wall had been raised against him. The lower North, stretching from New Jersey to Iowa, had given the New Yorker only 3½ votes out of

170. Lincoln, on the other hand, had received 62, with promises of more to come.

The second ballot followed immediately, and this time New England cast 33 votes for Seward, 36 for Lincoln. Once again its trend held for the whole convention as Pennsylvania led a shift to Lincoln which brought him almost even with Seward, 184½ to 181. Excitement was intense in the Wigwam as the clerk called the roll of states once more. Now Seward's New England total fell to 31, while Lincoln's rose prophetically to 42—more than half. And as the balloting proceeded, the sectional wall remained firmly intact, for Seward could still muster only 7 votes from the entire lower North, compared with Lincoln's 142½. When the totals were finally announced, Lincoln stood within 1½ votes of victory. Four delegates from Ohio quickly scrambled aboard the band wagon, and the deed was done. The rail splitter from Illinois had been nominated for the presidency. Outside, the city began its wild celebration, and the name "Lincoln" flashed along telegraph wires across the country. The Seward men were stunned not only by defeat but by the swiftness with which it had come. They walked, Halstead recorded, "from the slaughterhouse, more ashamed than embittered."

Much has been written about the shrewd tactics of Lincoln's managers and particularly about the lavish promises regarding cabinet posts and other appointments with which they lured delegates to their side. The nature, extent, and significance of these transactions is a matter of considerable dispute among historians, but in any case it might be well to remember that the Seward forces had just as many offices to peddle and something else besides—financial support in the various state elections. Similarly, the influence of the pro-Lincoln galleries should not be overestimated. In the vice-presidential contest, after all, the crowd shouted for Cassius M. Clay, but the prize went to Hannibal Hamlin. The convention was neither bought nor stampeded. The very pattern of voting reveals a hardheaded decision that the leading candidate could not win and must give way to someone who could. Yet in nominating the more "available" Lincoln, the Republicans did not compromise themselves or their objectives. In fact, without fully realizing it, they had selected a man whose moral fiber was tougher than Seward's.

VI

Back in 1854, the men calling themselves Republicans had constituted the radical wing of the anti-Nebraska coalition. Then a more moderate element had entered the picture and directed the work of effective organization. By 1858, some of its leaders were disposed to broaden the base of the party and reconstruct it along more conservative lines. If Republicanism had retained its pristine character, it probably would not have come into power. If, on the other hand, the party had followed the course marked out by Greeley, secession just might have been prevented, or at least postponed. But in choosing the middle way, in nominating an Abraham Lincoln, the Republicans made themselves both invincible in the North and unacceptable in the deep South. And the gloomy certainty with which many Southerners anticipated Lincoln's election during the summer of 1860 gave secessionist leaders all the more time to prepare for action.

Southern apprehensions, although fed by hysteria, were to some extent rooted in reality. For there was an unmistakable ambivalence at the core of Republicanism, well exemplified in Lincoln's contemplation of "ultimate extinction" while guaranteeing the security of slavery where it already existed. Furthermore, dimly visible behind this aggressive new political machine were the mobilizing forces of an economic order which likewise seemed inimical to the Southern way of life. The Republican Party in 1860, although posing no great immediate threat to the slaveholding society of the South, nevertheless carried within it an implication of that society's doom. In their eventual decision to withdraw from the emerging newer nation symbolized by Lincoln, Southerners were in effect attempting to hold back a future that appeared to have no place for them.

ROBERT W. JOHANNSEN

III

Douglas at Charleston

No American political convention has ever held so much meaning for party and nation as that conclave of determined Democrats which gathered in Charleston, South Carolina, in April, 1860, to nominate a candidate for the presidential office. Upon the decision at Charleston rested not only the future of the Democratic Party but also the continued existence of the Union. The meeting was the sectional conflict in microcosm. All the forces of sectional animosity that had been building up between the North and the South for over a decade were focused on those ten fateful days. When the convention adjourned, its business unfinished, the party of Andrew Jackson had been reduced to a shambles and the fate of the nation had been sealed.

The central figure in the struggle was Senator Stephen A. Douglas of Illinois. Douglas, according to a young Cincinnati journalist covering the convention, "was the pivot individual" of the meeting. "Every delegate," he wrote, "was for or against him. Every motion meant to nominate him or not to nominate him. Every parliamentary war was *pro* or *con* Douglas." Around Douglas raged the battle which ultimately laid the party low. To many in the party he was the only candidate capable of carrying the Democratic banner to victory in the November election. Many others were equally sincere in their assertions that the future of the party demanded Douglas' rejection by the convention. There was much talk of principle on both sides.

Stephen A. Douglas had occupied the political limelight for a decade, unquestionably the most controversial figure in American politics. Twice before he had sought the presidential nomination of his party but each time he was passed over in favor of a less controversial individual. In 1852, he was defeated by his youth and the overly active exertions of some of his political friends; in 1856, he conceded the nomination to James Buchanan when it was demonstrated that the latter was the clear choice of a majority of the convention. The dominating political struggle in American politics during the fifties was over the expansion of slavery into the territories of the West, an issue which became increasingly abstract in its application to the actual circumstances of Western settlement and development. As it became more abstract, it also became more explosive, until it involved the political, economic, and social differences dividing the two great sections of the nation.

Douglas' name was synonymous with "popular sovereignty," a solution to the problem of slavery's expansion which he hoped would heal the wounds in the Democratic Party as well as restore sectional harmony to the nation. Denying that Congress should or could exercise legislative authority over the internal workings of the Western territories, Douglas defined popular sovereignty as the "right of the people of an organized Territory, under the Constitution and laws of the United States, to govern themselves in respect to their own internal policy and domestic affairs." In actuality, it had come to mean little more than the right of a territory to legislate for itself on the slavery question. Vital to Douglas' principle was his insistence that the right of the territory to exercise its power was determined and tempered by the United States Constitution. On the question of Constitutional interpretation, however, the differences between Douglas and his opponents were deep and formidable. Douglas was assailed by both the Republicans and the Southern members of his own party.

Douglas' doctrine was, in some respects, nebulous and ambiguous. Its ambiguity had been carefully preserved in the national platform of the Democratic Party formulated in 1856 at the Cincinnati convention. The framers of the Cincinnati platform recognized two conflicting interpretations of the extent to which people in a territory could deal with slavery, but glossed over these differences in order to maintain unity in the Democratic Party. Douglas argued that power to determine the status of slavery in the territories could be exercised by the territorial legislatures; Southerners, on the other hand, insisted that this power could be wielded only when the territory was moving into statehood. The Cincinnati platform was sufficiently vague to allow both constructions.

Although Douglas had received the support of the Southern slave states in his bid for the presidential nomination in 1856, his actions during the following four years alienated that section. In his interpretation of the Cincinnati platform he insisted more firmly on his brand of popular sovereignty. In 1857, in what was perhaps the most significant act of his career, Douglas strongly opposed the proslave Kansas Lecompton Constitution as a travesty on popular sovereignty, as an attempt to impose the institution of slavery on Kansas against the wishes of a majority of its population. His opposition was a gesture of open defiance not only against the South but also against the Buchanan administration, an act for which neither the South nor the President ever forgave him. To the South, Douglas demonstrated his untrustworthiness as a spokesman and defender of Southern interests. In 1858, the Illinois Senator compounded his felony in the eyes of the South when he further clarified his position in his famous debates with Abraham Lincoln. During the Freeport debate he maintained that, the Supreme Court to the contrary notwithstanding, a territorial legislature could, by "unfriendly legislation," effectively bar the introduction of slavery. To be sure, Douglas had made such statements before, but never before had they been so explicit and so widely publicized. That Douglas had become completely unacceptable to the South and to the administration was indicated soon after the conclusion of the debates, when, at the opening of the second session of the Thirty-fifth Congress, the Democratic caucus removed him from his influential position as chairman of the Senate Committee on Territories for his espousal of what was called the "Freeport heresy." Through the removal, Douglas' enemies gave notice of their determination to read the Little Giant out of the Democratic Party.

The attacks by Southerners on Douglas' position only stiffened his devotion to popular sovereignty. In late February, 1859, he was called to account in the Senate by three of his Southern foes, Albert Gallatin Brown, Jefferson Davis, and James Stephen Green, and in a running debate forced to expound his views and to defend his doctrine of "unfriendly legislation." A short while later, he confided in a letter to an Illinois supporter that he would not make peace with his enemies, nor did he intend "to make a concession of one iota of principle." Douglas had his eye fixed on the coming presidential election. In June, he wrote an Iowa newspaper editor that he would accept the presidential nomination in 1860 only if the convention endorsed his position. Under no circumstances, he declared, would he accept the nomination on a platform including the revival of the African slave trade, a Congressional slave code for the territories, or "the doctrine that the Constitution of the United States either establishes or prohibits slavery in the Territories beyond the power of the people legally to control it as other property."

To a Georgian in September, Douglas reiterated his support for the Cincinnati platform, as interpreted by him, and announced his readiness to accept it once again at the Charleston convention. "We stand by the Cincinnati Platform according to its obvious meaning," he wrote, "and are ready to reaffirm it at Charleston without the change of a word, and will then give it the same construction we have always given it. If this is not satisfactory to some of our Southern friends we shall regret but cannot avoid it." No clearer warning could have been made to the South. The Cincinnati platform, having served as party cement before, could do so again, but only with a clear understanding and acceptance of the interpretation Douglas placed upon it. "I firmly believe I am right," he continued, "and cannot change my opinions at this late day even to be President."

The final stroke in Douglas' preconvention strategy came in September, 1859. Not satisfied with his statements made in the heat of Senate debate or in private letters to his anxious supporters, the Little Giant determined to settle finally any doubts that might still persist regarding his views. In that month, he published his most complete exposition of popular sovereignty in *Harper's Magazine,* in an article entitled "The Dividing Line Between Federal and Local Authority: Popular Sovereignty in the Territories." In his statement, Douglas sought to ground his doctrine firmly on historical precedent and Constitutional authority. The article fell like a bombshell on the South. Douglas' chances for strong Southern support in the Charleston convention were reduced to the vanishing point. To one Alabama Congressman, the article had placed Douglas "outside the pale of the party." A Georgia Senator declared that acceptance of Douglas now would be suicidal for the South. The Richmond *Enquirer* regarded the essay as the "most dangerous phase which anti-slavery agitation has yet assumed." Douglas' nomination, it was said, would be an insult to the South "which she must resent by defeating him at all hazards." Douglas' statements strengthened him in the North, but to the Southern politicians who still

felt the sting of his anti-Lecompton stand and his Freeport enunciation, his *Harper's* essay was the crowning
infamy. A showdown became inevitable.

II

As Douglas prepared to do battle for the Charleston
nomination his Southern antagonists moved to resist his
aspirations. It was clear that Douglas enjoyed considerable support from the Southern people, including the editors of several key Southern newspapers, but it was equally
clear that he was unacceptable to the section's political
leaders. Goaded by Douglas' insistence on a popular sovereignty platform, Southern leaders rejected any notion that
the 1856 Cincinnati platform would be acceptable in the
1860 campaign. The Cincinnati platform was a sham,
a deception; its ambiguity could no longer serve the party
nor could it be relied upon to protect Southern slave interests in the territories. There must be, they said, "no
Douglas dodges—no double constructions." The South
must assume an unequivocal position against the
"heresies" of the Illinois Senator. The answer was found
in a new, more extreme program—the demand for a
Congressional slave code in the territories. The slave code
marked the desperation of Southern leaders. It was an
emphatic response to the challenge of Douglas' construction of the Cincinnati platform and a protest against
the Freeport Doctrine, which had robbed the South of
victory in the Dred Scott decision. The defeat of the
Lecompton movement in Kansas also demonstrated the
need for new foolproof guarantees for slavery in the territories. The South feared not only Douglas but also
the North. Northern political strength would be aug-

mented by the census of 1860 and the South's minority status would become even more pronounced. In adopting the slave code demand, Southerners unabashedly accepted the principle of Congressional control over the institution, a principle which they now shared with the Republicans.

The new Southern demand was formally announced in February, 1860, in a series of resolutions introduced into the United States Senate by Jefferson Davis. The resolutions provided a complete statement of the Southern position. The fourth resolution denied that either Congress or a territorial legislature, "whether by direct legislation or legislation of an indirect and unfriendly character," could impair the right of a person to hold a slave in a territory. In the absence of adequate protection to slave property in the territories, by the national executive or judiciary or by the territorial government, Congress, according to the fifth resolution, was obligated to intervene for the protection of the institution. The Southern interpretation of the Cincinnati platform was emphasized once again; the people of a territory had no power to determine the status of slavery until they formed a state constitution. The Davis resolutions were further discussed in March, 1860, but no attempt was made to pass them before the meeting of the Charleston convention. They stood as advice to the platform committee of the convention.

If the slave code demand served as advice to the party delegates who would gather in Charleston, it also served as a warning and ultimatum to the supporters of Stephen A. Douglas. The Davis resolutions represented the only terms acceptable to the South. Harmony in the convention would depend on Douglas' acquiescence in the Southern position, a development that could hardly be foreseen. The ultimatum had been served on Douglas as early as September, 1859, when Senator Albert Gallatin Brown of Mississippi wrote to the Little Giant, "The South will demand at Charleston a platform explicitly declaring that slave property is entitled in the Territories and on the high seas to the same protection that is given to any other and every other species of property—and failing to get it, she will retire from the convention." Brown's threat would prove an accurate forecast. Far more serious and ominous for the future existence of the Democratic Party was the course pursued by the Alabama state convention in January, 1860. Under the leadership of the "fire-eater," William Lowndes Yancey, the convention endorsed the slave code principle and instructed its delegates to the national convention to withdraw from its deliberations if this principle should not be incorporated in the party platform. Yancey himself was to lead the Alabama delegation at Charleston. Other Southern state conventions gave the slave code strong endorsement. It became increasingly clear that the unity of the party would depend upon the acceptance of what became known as the "Alabama Platform." Alabama would not be alone if a walkout should occur. On the eve of the Charleston meeting, Douglas was informed that the Texas delegates were pledged secretly to withdraw if the Southern demands were not met. There was ample evidence that this strategy had support in other Southern delegations.

The slave code demand marked the determination of the South to mold the Democratic Party to her own pattern and to formulate a new policy that would guarantee, without equivocation, Southern rights in the territories against the ambiguities of popular sovereignty and the anticipated onslaughts of the Northern slavery restrictionists. But the slave code was also more than this. Douglas' enemies, Northern as well as Southern, saw in the slave code an effective means for securing Douglas' rejection by the Democratic convention. Douglas, by his own statement, would never consent to stand on a slave code platform. Indeed, his political future in the North depended upon a complete repudiation of the Southern proposal. To conclude, however, that the Southern ultimatum was primarily a pretext, a device to defeat Douglas, is to overlook the grim determination of Southern leaders to secure new guarantees for the expansion of their "peculiar institution" and for their continued exercise of political leadership within the party and the nation. Douglas was unacceptable to Southern and administration Democrats for his unforgivable defiance of the party leadership in the Lecompton crisis but he was also unacceptable for the position he represented on the question of slavery in the territories. Southern radicals, commented one observer at the convention, would be less insistent on the platform if they could be certain that Douglas would be defeated for the nomination. For Douglas *was* a platform; popular sovereignty and the Illinois Senator had by 1860 become indistinguishable.

The lines of battle were drawn long before the Charleston convention opened. Like the rays of the sun through a magnifying glass, the sectional differences were brought to a focus on the attempt of this last

Robert W. Johannsen

national political party to agree on a presidential candidate. A conflagration resulted. There was no possibility for compromise and no possible result other than the destruction of the party unless one or the other of the two groups should beat a full retreat. The prospect of such a retreat was remote indeed. Northern and Northwestern delegates were as adamant in their refusal to bow to the slave code ultimatum as were the Southerners in insisting upon its acceptance. Acquiescence in the Southern demands would mean political suicide in the North; political survival depended upon an acceptance of Douglas and popular sovereignty. To many of Douglas' supporters a showdown with the South was imminent and even desirable. They smarted under repeated Republican charges of subservience to the slave power; a surrender to the South was unthinkable. Early in 1859, over a year before the Charleston meeting, one of Douglas' close Illinois associates advised, "We are not in a condition to carry another ounce of Southern weight." To accede to the slave code, he continued, "would be *inexplicable inconsistency,* invoking the fatal acknowledgement *as error* all our preconceived notions of the right and capacity of the people to regulate their domestic affairs in their own way." Feeble, but hopeful, signs of a reconciliation between Douglas and his Southern colleagues in the Democratic Party had appeared during the session of Congress which met in December, 1859, when there were indications that Douglas' anti-Lecompton followers were once again in good party standing. However, a small group of radical, ultra Southerners demonstrated their conviction that party defeat was preferable to cooperation with Douglas men—an attitude that cast an ominous shadow on the Charleston convention. Davis' slave code resolutions ended all hopes that the party's wounds might be healed. A pro-Douglas Maryland delegate assured the Illinois Senator that "there can arise no contingency in the Convention when your friends will agree to vote for any other man than yourself. The time for compromise and postponement upon that point has passed and so sure as the Convention will make a nomination—so sure will you be the man."

Robert Barnwell Rhett, fiery Southern radical, secessionist, and editor of the Charleston *Mercury*, refused to wait for the convention to meet before pronouncing an obituary over the Democratic Party. Exactly one week before the convention was scheduled to open, Rhett commented, "The Democratic party, as a party, based upon principles, is dead. It exists now, only as a powerful faction. It has not one single principle common to its members North and South." As for the proper course the South should follow, Rhett advised, "Firmness is the dictate of necessity. She must cease fraternization with any who deny her essential rights, and the great principles of the Democratic party." Yet Douglas refused to give up hope. In February, he had written confidently to a member of the New York delegation that "there will be no serious difficulty in the South." He was fully aware that his nomination would depend on Southern support, but every mail brought reassurances of his strength with the Southern people.

III

For Douglas and the Democratic Party no choice of convention site could have been more unfortunate than that of Charleston, South Carolina. The selection had been made by the Democratic national committee in 1856 in order to promote party harmony. The members of the committee could hardly have foreseen how far their strategy would miss the mark. Charleston, a center of proud ultra Southernism, was for Douglas the heart of enemy territory. It was a stronghold of secessionism, paced by the "fire-eater" Rhett, and this characteristic augured ill for Douglas, the Democratic Party, and the Union. Both sides were cognizant of the importance to their respective causes of what they termed the "outside pressure." The choice of Charleston placed the advantage in this regard squarely with the Southern leaders. For this reason, many in the Douglas camp felt that the convention site should be changed. George N. Sanders, fearing administration pressure against Douglas as well as a hostile atmosphere, wrote that the farther the meeting was held from Washington the better off Douglas would be. He suggested New Orleans, since "it is more accessible to your friends than any other place." Others maintained that Baltimore would present a more congenial environment to Douglas' efforts.

Failing to secure a change, the Douglas men regarded it as an absolute necessity that large numbers from the Northwestern states should go to Charleston to offset the Southern advantage. Douglas spelled out his wishes in a letter to Charles H. Lanphier, editor of the pro-Douglas *Illinois State Register* and a leading wire-puller in the Douglas camp. The Illinois state convention, he proposed, should "appoint as many assistant or consulting delegates as it chooses. . . . In this way all of our friends can go in a quasi official capacity, and the more the better. It may not be politic to announce to the world that a large number is expected to go, but it is important that all our leading men in the State should be at Charleston."

Northern delegates were doubtful of Charleston for reasons other than the atmosphere of hostility which they knew they would encounter there. For weeks before the convention opened, rumors flew through the North that hotel accommodations in the Southern city left much to be desired and that the hotelkeepers were determined to charge exorbitant prices for the available space. Such rumors discouraged many who might otherwise have made the trip. From Indiana came word that the high prices at Charleston would "have an effect upon some delegates to keep them away from the convention." An Illinois delegate feared that "owing to the uncertainty of getting quarters at Charleston . . . there will not be a large delegation from Ill." A member of the Minnesota delegation commented that "the hospitality of our chivalry loving & generous Southerners is seriously damaged by their attempts at extortion."

Charleston was difficult of access and many of the delegates complained of the long and exhausting journey necessary to reach the city. F. O. Prince, a Massachusetts delegate, in a letter to Adele Cutts Douglas written three days after the convention opened, reported:

I have never been taught to believe in eternal punishment, but the journey here has led me to recognize the contrary "platform," to use the term now current, since it has appeared to me, that those who were instrumental in locating the convention here can only be adequately punished therefor by *Brimstone* and *Caloric ad infinitum.* Not that I complain of Charleston, for it is a most charming city, and the Charlestonese incarnate every quality that graces humanity—most especially, beauty, wit & hospitality . . . but my objection in coming here, is on account of the fatigues & miseries of the journey. Such slow coaches—facetiously termed steam cars! Such abominable hotels! . . . If Mr. Douglas is not nominated pretty soon, I shall become a *pauper.*

Some delegates sought to beat the high prices by providing their own accommodations. The Indiana delegation, for example, announced its intention to pitch tents in Charleston, a plan soon abandoned. Other delegations chartered steamers which would serve not only to carry them to the convention but would also be floating hotels while there. The Pennsylvania delegation arrived on board the *Keystone State,* well stocked with 500 barrels of domestic liquor and 300 kegs of lager beer. New Yorkers arrived on the *Nashville,* equally well prepared to withstand the rigors of a nominating convention, with the addition, it was said, of a contingent of "amiable females." A third steamer, the *S. R. Spaulding,* housed a group from Boston. None, however, had anticipated the length of the deliberations and after five days these delegations found themselves paying handsomely for the comfort of their accommodations.

Others were similarly caught short by the prolonged discussions. At the end of the first week, Murat Halstead, a newspaperman covering the convention, reported, "A great calamity has come upon the Ohio delegation. Their private whiskey, of which they laid in a supply supposed to be equal to all emergencies, the nomination of Douglas included, gave out this morning." Nor were the Ohioans alone in their distress. The Kentucky whiskey, Halstead asserted, was "nearly all gone." The Douglas delegations from the Northwestern states took up quarters in Hibernia Hall, where 132 cots were crammed into a single large room on the second floor. At Mills House there were four or five persons to a room. Still, fewer persons than had been anticipated arrived in the convention city. The crowded, cramped quarters, the rapidly diminishing stocks of whiskey, the unseasonable heat (the temperature hovered in the high nineties during the first days of the convention), and the prospect of a long session resulted in frayed nerves and hair-trigger tempers. The combination did not bode well for the cause of party harmony.

IV

The convention opened on Douglas' forty-seventh birthday, but the occasion was hardly a festive one for the Little Giant. Douglas himself remained in Washington during the sitting of the convention, in close touch with his lieutenants at Charleston. Leading the fight for Douglas was William A. Richardson, large, broad-shouldered, and powerful. He had been elected to Congress from Douglas' own Quincy, Illinois, district when the latter was elevated to the Senate, and in the House of Representatives became Douglas' most loyal champion. In 1856, he had managed Douglas' campaign in the Cincinnati convention. Richardson had a voice, it was said, that rose over the clamor of the convention like a fire bell, and when he spoke he commanded universal attention. He was recognized as the strong man of the Northwest and won wide respect for his shrewd and forceful manipulation of the Douglas strategy. His task was one of gigantic proportions. It was clear, and widely recognized, that Douglas was the favorite of a majority of the delegates but no one would concede him the two-thirds majority necessary for the nomination. The game of Douglas' followers was to remain calm and even concilia- tory in their attitude toward the South, a tack that proved difficult for some delegates to maintain. A member of the Illinois delegation complained to Douglas of "the bitter- ness of some of our Southern opponents. They go so far as to call us all abolitionists and say we had better stay at home and attend the Chicago convention where we legitimately belong. I assure you it is with great diffi- culty we can keep cool but we do so and with kind words turn away strife."

Representing the Buchanan administration was the powerful Senator from Louisiana, John Slidell, hard-work- ing, resolute, and dangerous, unflinching in his deter- mination to secure Douglas' downfall. His arrival from Washington just before the convention opened created a sensation among the delegates; his appearance, it was said, "means war to the knife." Although not a delegate, his influence at Charleston was strong. Assisting Slidell was Indiana's heavy, businesslike Senator Jesse Bright, whose hatred for the Little Giant was "the strongest passion of his soul." The administration was not particular about the platform; its main purpose was to defeat Doug- las.

The lion of the convention, however, was William Lowndes Yancey, leader of the Alabama delegation and the "prince of the fire-eaters." Mild-mannered, gentle- manly, and sincere, he was, perhaps, the most powerful man in the convention and certainly the most popular with Charleston's citizens. A captivating speaker, Yancey was always greeted with huge ovations from the galleries.

During the preliminaries of organization, he played a quiet, passive role, "always wearing a genuinely good-humored smile and looking as if nothing in the world could disturb the equanimity of his spirits." He waited in the wings for the crisis which would be his cue for action. Yancey's course was clear, and it would not be an exaggeration to say that much of the fate of the Democratic Party rested in his hands. The crisis he awaited was brought one step closer two days before the convention opened when the delegations from six Southern states met in caucus and agreed to stand on Yancey's Alabama platform. If Douglas should be nominated, the Southern delegates announced, they would bolt the convention. The decision, it was said, fell on the Douglas camp like a "thunderbolt."

In spite of these signs, the first actions of the convention were favorable to Douglas. The delegations from Illinois and New York, both pro-Douglas, were challenged by rival groups, headed by Isaac Cook, erstwhile Chicago Postmaster and inveterate foe of Douglas, and Fernando Wood, former Mayor of New York city. The chairman of the Democratic national committee, David Smalley of Vermont, whose task it was to set the convention in motion, denied tickets to the Cook and Wood delegations, thus preventing them from taking seats in the convention hall. Smalley, a staunch Douglas man, had attended school with the Senator when both were youths in Vermont. T. B. Flournoy, a Douglas man from Arkansas, was nominated and elected temporary president of the convention. In the first test vote of the meeting, Smalley's action was upheld and the Douglas delegations from Illinois and New York were accorded places on the credentials and organization committees, and two days later the credentials committee reported in favor of their being permanently seated in the body. In a second test of strength, the convention approved a Douglas-sponsored rule change which would enable delegates in uninstructed delegations to cast their individual votes. This was a distinct triumph for the Douglas forces, silencing the anti-Douglas minorities in instructed delegations and freeing the pro-Douglas minorities in uninstructed delegations. Douglas' only setback in the preliminaries of the convention came with the choice of Caleb Cushing of Massachusetts, an anti-Douglas, proadministration man, for the permanent presidency of the convention.

In the face of these setbacks, the resistance of the administration-Southern coalition to Douglas' candidacy hardened. The actions of the first two days had revealed not only the solidarity and discipline of the Douglas majority but also the weakness of the ultra Southern position. Southern delegates, moreover, proved unable to agree on a candidate of their own. Their success could only be achieved by forcing an issue over the platform. At the end of the first day of the convention, a caucus of Southern delegates met for a second time and agreed to stand on Jefferson Davis' slave code resolutions in the formulation of the platform. The administration spokesmen strongly advised that the platform be adopted before the nomination. The slave code could thus become the weapon by which Douglas would be cut down. As deliberations resumed on the second day, Halstead noted, "There is an impression prevalent this morning that the Convention is destined to explode in a grand row. . . . There is tumult and war in prospect."

On the afternoon of the second day, the convention made the fatal decision to adopt a platform before balloting for a presidential candidate. Strangely enough, the proposal received the united support of both Douglas and Southern men and passed the convention by an overwhelming margin. Both sides claimed the decision as a victory; each was confident that it could secure its own platform. The outlook was brighter for the Southern leaders than it was for Douglas. On the resolutions committee, where voting would be by states, the South could count on the votes of the fifteen slave states and the two free states of Oregon and California, a majority of the committee. Not all Douglas men, on the other hand, were convinced of the wisdom of their strategy. Charles E. Stuart, delegate from Michigan and a leader of the Douglas group, preferred to nominate a candidate first, but he acquiesced in the wishes of his colleagues. The chances for success seemed good to Stuart, although he conceded that there were men in the convention who were determined to resist their efforts "by any and all means in their power"; men who were, he noted, "potent for mischief."

This decision to write the platform first sealed the fate of the convention. Neither side was willing to give way on its fundamental position regarding slavery in the territories. The Douglas men in the convention expressed a willingness to support an ambiguous platform, one that would allow the Southern leaders to argue their interpretation before their constituents but always with the understanding that Douglas himself would continue to press his popular sovereignty doctrine. Members of the Douglas camp expressed full satisfaction with a re-adoption of the Cincinnati platform, with the Dred Scott decision tacked on "as a tail to the kite," and some of Douglas' influential Southern supporters believed this to be the best formula. Douglas himself had telegraphed his supporters to yield this much, but no more. But Southern leaders recalled only too well Douglas' repeated statements that the court decision in no wise affected the operation of popular sovereignty and his more serious pronouncement at Freeport, which nullified the effect of the decision. The offer was a hollow concession. At the same time, Northern delegates reiterated their opposition to the slave code and some of them threatened to bolt the convention on their part if the South should have its way. The decision to make the platform before the nomination meant that the disruption of the party would arrive sooner than most had expected, that the final struggle would be waged over the platform and not the nomination, and that the importance of the platform to the campaign against Douglas would be exaggerated. "Here, then," commented Halstead, "is the 'irrepressible conflict'—a conflict between enduring forces."

The resolutions committee, whose task it was to report a platform to the convention, began its deliberations on the evening of the second day and continued in session until the morning of the fifth day. In the meantime, the delegates bided their time. Many of them, convinced that they had discovered the solution to the party's problems, introduced resolutions which were dutifully referred to the platform committee, until one delegate, reflecting the weariness of the convention, moved that further resolutions be referred to the committee without reading. As the committee continued to discuss the platform, the sense of crisis heightened among the delegates. Rumors of the committee's inability to agree upon a single set of resolutions sped through the hall, and some feared that the committee would be unable to report at all. The hopelessness of its task became apparent. As one reporter wrote, the committee "must bring in a subterfuge, or throw a bombshell."

A bombshell it was. Not one, but three platforms were submitted. The chairman of the committee, a delegate from North Carolina, presented the majority report. The Cincinnati platform was affirmed, but several new explanatory resolutions were added, two of which were designed to render it unequivocally in favor of slavery in the territories. Popular sovereignty, the power of a territorial legislature to determine the status of slavery, was forcefully denied and the slave code was endorsed. A minority report, representing the views of the Douglas members of the committee, also affirmed the Cincinnati platform but added, in what was intended as a concession to the South, that all questions pertaining to the rights of property in the territories should be referred to the judiciary. The Democratic Party, the report continued, would be "pledged to abide by and faithfully carry out such determination of these questions as has been or may be made by the Supreme Court of the United States." This was an implication, at least, that Douglas was willing to stand on the Dred Scott decision. A third proposal, submitted by Benjamin F. Butler of Massachusetts, simply endorsed the Cincinnati platform without the addition of any explanatory resolutions.

Each of the reports was defended by spokesmen from the committee. Speaking for the Douglas report, Ohio's Henry B. Payne made more explicit the implication in the platform. Douglas would, he emphasized, support the Dred Scott decision and would abide by any future judicial pronouncements on the question of slavery in the territories. This, he felt, was all the South could ask of him.

The presentation of the platforms produced the crisis for which Yancey had waited. In an hour-and-a-half speech to the ringing applause of delegates and visitors, the Alabama leader defended the ultra Southern position and mounted a vigorous attack against Douglas and his doctrines. He inveighed against Douglas' record in the Kansas question, his treachery in the Lecompton struggle, and his oft-repeated assertion that most of the Dred Scott decision was mere *obiter dicta*. The South, he maintained, could no longer trust the Illinois Senator and new guarantees of Southern rights were necessary. Defeat upon principle, Yancey declared, was preferable to a victory achieved on ambiguous issues. Yancey's address, interrupted frequently by shouts of approbation and stamping of feet, was clearly the high point of the convention. Senator George E. Pugh of Ohio undertook the Douglas rebuttal. Heated to the point of anger, Pugh denounced the Southern demand that the Northern Democracy bow to the new ultimatum. "Gentlemen of the South," he roared, "you mistake us—you mistake us—we will not do it." The showdown had at last arrived.

Events moved rapidly following the presentation of the controversial platforms. After a night spent in frantic maneuvering, a desperation attempt to avert an explosion was undertaken. Pennsylvania's Senator William Bigler moved that the majority and minority reports be recommitted to the resolutions committee and proposed a new set of resolutions as a compromise formula. The motion won by the bare majority of a single vote, against the strong opposition of the Douglas supporters. The Douglasites, however, succeeded in defeating Bigler's formula. The resolutions committee made a second report later in the day, once again submitting three platforms. The majority report restated the Southern position in slightly altered wording, incorporating elements of Bigler's proposals. The basic ideas remained the same. The minority report was similarly revised in wording, but not in sense. Butler once again proposed a simple reaffirmation of the Cincinnati platform, gaining on this occasion the support of three Douglas members of the committee. In spite of the maneuver, the lines were still drawn as rigidly as before. The disruption had only been postponed.

An immediate vote on the platform was averted, and after a period of extremely confusing parliamentary wrangling, Cushing threatened to leave the chair and abandon the convention. At this the delegates agreed to adjourn. The next day was Sunday, an opportunity for the convention to take stock of itself and for the leaders of the two opposing forces to try their powers of persuasion on the wavering delegates.

Monday, April 30, was the last day for a united Democratic Party. The delegates gathered in the convention hall, disheartened and discouraged at the prospects of mending the breach between Douglas and the South. The sorry spectacle presented by the party to the nation would, in any case, defeat them in November, no matter what the outcome of the struggle. Butler's proposal, the Cincinnati platform pure and unalloyed, was first rejected. A motion to substitute the minority, or Douglas, report for the majority report was then adopted, and the delegates girded themselves for the final crisis—the vote on the minority report as the platform of the Democratic Party. Tensions that had been building for days now reached their peak. Each section of the report, it was decided, would be voted upon separately. The first, affirming the Cincinnati platform, was accepted. The voting was interspersed with explanations, threats, and warnings. Douglas men pleaded for party unity; Southerners denounced what they called the "Cincinnati swindle" and asserted that they could never agree to stand on a court decision that was variously interpreted. As the vote commenced on the second section of the minority platform— that pledging the party to abide by the decisions of the Supreme Court on questions of slavery in the territories— the Douglas men made their final move. Richardson unsuccessfully sought the floor for an announcement, but as the balloting continued his strategy became clear. The section was to be dropped and the Douglasites would fall back on a simple reaffirmation of the Cincinnati platform without explanation. This was their final retreat but it was of no avail. It is significant that the delegates from seven Southern states refused to vote on the section. The remaining planks of the minority platform, dealing with the Pacific railroad, the rights of naturalized citizens, the enforcement of the Fugitive Slave Law, and the acquisition of Cuba, were also adopted without their participation. Charles E. Stuart, obviously angered at the failure of the South to accept what was intended as an olive branch, concluded with an inflammatory speech that only served to irritate the Southern delegates further. Following Stuart's speech, delegations from Alabama, Mississippi,

Louisiana, South Carolina, Florida, Texas, and Arkansas withdrew from the convention amid impassioned oratory and the applause of the galleries. The next morning, the Georgia delegation walked out. The final blow had been delivered and the party lay prostrate.

The remaining sessions of the convention were anti-climactic. Balloting for a presidential candidate began, but not until after a brief, but bitter, skirmish over the two-thirds rule. The powerful and somewhat enigmatic New York delegation assumed the role of peacemaker. In consultation with delegates from the border slave states, the New Yorkers supported a resolution that would require the nominee to receive two-thirds of the vote of the full convention, rather than simply two-thirds of those votes which remained in the hall. The adoption of the resolution was a defeat for Douglas' managers, dashing their hopes that the Little Giant might be nominated easily and quickly following the Southern withdrawal. The New York move, it was thought, would force the Douglas supporters to accept a compromise candidate who might reunite the convention. The New York compromisers also attacked the stalemate on the platform. Working with the same border state delegations, the New Yorkers proposed a new resolution on the slavery problem, a bridge over which the seceders might return to the fold. Introduced by a Tennessean, it became known as the "Tennessee Platform." In actuality it was nothing more than a rewording, in milder form, of the Southern slave code proposition. Richardson emphatically informed the compromisers that there would be no surrender on the Douglas side. The Douglasites answered by staging their own coup. After several futile ballots, the convention was adjourned, to meet again in Baltimore on June 18. The Douglas leadership appealed to the citizens of the states whose delegates had withdrawn and urged them to select new delegations for the Baltimore meeting.

V

The withdrawal of the eight Southern states staggered the Douglas men. Most of them had accepted the secession of a few delegates, notably the Alabama group, as inevitable, but had regarded the possibility of a "little eruption" as an asset to their campaign. The withdrawal of a few of the Southern extremists, they argued, would enhance their chances for winning over the remaining Southern delegates. A limited withdrawal would also strengthen them in the North. Administration leaders saw through this strategy and sought to persuade the Southern hotheads to remain in the convention even after the adoption of the Douglas platform. Douglas, they were convinced, could never secure the nomination of a united convention. The two-thirds rule could be used effectively to strike down the Illinois Senator. The real target, they maintained, was not the platform but Douglas himself. For a time it seemed as if this tactic would be successful. On Sunday, the day before the explosion, it was widely rumored that only Yancey's delegation would withdraw, and there were reports that Yancey himself had been persuaded to remain in the convention.

The convention was a tragedy of miscalculations. The politicians, who believed themselves the masters of the situation, had, in fact, lost control of it. The solidarity of the Southern politicians against Douglas and their determination to end all ambiguities on the slavery question had not been anticipated by Douglas' managers. Douglas was laboring under an exaggerated impression of his own strength in the South. Southern delegates, he felt, would not dare follow a course which would result in their repudiation at home. He did not reckon with the deep distrust felt toward him by administration and Southern leaders or with the personal antagonisms which his Lecompton course two years before had aroused.

Southern delegates were aware that Douglas commanded the support of a majority of the convention, that even if Douglas could not secure the nomination for himself he had the strength to prevent the nomination of anyone more acceptable to the South. In any case, the South would occupy a subordinate place in the party. The showdown had to come on the platform. Douglas' concessions on the minority platform were not really concessions at all. His retreat on the Supreme Court section was not a surrender. The platform, as finally approved, affirmed the Cincinnati platform without explanation, exactly that proposed by Douglas before the convention. The weight of the "outside pressure" was wholly on the side of the seceders. Their every move was greeted with frenzied enthusiasm by the Charleston citizens who crowded the galleries. It was difficult indeed for the Southern delegates to resist this encouragement.

The belief that their withdrawal would force new concessions from the convention was never lost among the seceded delegates. They went through the motions of organization, then settled back to await the action of the convention. Some confidently expected that the hand of peace and friendship would be extended, but it never came. Instead came the unexpected news that the convention had adjourned without making a nomination, to resume its deliberations six weeks hence in Baltimore. The seceders would have to go home to convince their constituents that the action they had taken was right.

Douglas was the rock on which the last national political party foundered, but to minimize the importance of the platform in the disruption of the party is to ignore the Little Giant's commitment, both public and private, to popular sovereignty. His record, his popularity, and his increasing strength in the Democratic Party all demanded, for the South, an explicit statement of Southern principles. It is not correct to attribute the disruption solely to personal antagonisms. Following the explosion, Georgia's Senator Robert Toombs commented, "I am fully aware that personal hostilities and personal advantages are at the bottom of the strife; but there is a right and a wrong to the controversy for all that." Nor could Douglas have withdrawn from the struggle. If he had bowed out, the platform and candidate might reflect the Southern position, a position long hostile to his own. He would be forced to fight the ticket, if not as a Democrat, then as a Republican. The latter course was utterly repugnant to him. To acquiesce would be to lose all standing in the Democratic Party. He was convinced, and probably he was right, that he had the support of a majority of Democrats in the nation. His course in national politics demanded vindication. In 1858, he had been branded a heretic and every attempt was made to read him out of the party. His honor as well as his political future demanded an uncompromising stand at the convention. Finally, the careers of countless Northern politicians rode on the fortunes of the Illinois Senator; a surrender to the Southern demands would have betrayed his followers into the hands of their enemies. Too much had been conceded the South already. There is evidence that even if Douglas had decided to withdraw at Charleston, his supporters would have prevented his doing so. The Northwestern Democracy was in rebellion against the Southern leadership and was determined to stand fast.

With the destruction of the last national party at Charleston the nation itself was placed in peril. The safety of the Union depended upon the ability of the Democratic Party to adjust its differences and to present a united front in the November election. If the Democratic Party could not maintain its unity, then there was no hope for the nation. As the party was rendered impotent the days of national union were numbered. On the night of the withdrawal of the Southern delegates from the convention, thousands of Charlestonians gathered in the streets, raising a cry for "Yancey! Yancey!" The Alabaman obliged, and in a ringing speech, vindicated the Southern action, called for a vigorous defense of Southern rights, and urged that the South stand united against Northern aggressions. He concluded with the speculation that "perhaps even now, the pen of the historian was nibbed to write the story of a new revolution." At this point, the assembled multitude gave "three cheers for the Independent Southern Republic." This was the legacy of the Charleston convention.

WILLIAM E. BARINGER

IV

The Republican Triumph

For many Americans the campaign of 1860 was not unlike those which had preceded it. It confronted them with the usual obligation to observe candidates and issues so that they might render a suitable decision in November, quite certain that whoever won the election, the business of government would continue largely unaltered. True, there were four major candidates in the field instead of the customary two, and this alone was evidence that the nation's political parties were experiencing troublesome times. And one candidate, Abraham Lincoln, represented a purely sectional party—one with state organizations only in the North. His victory would represent the elevation of not only a party but also a geographical region over its opposition. Some Southerners had warned that they would regard a Republican victory as synonymous with conquest at the hands of an alien power—an extremity to be resisted by every available means.

Despite the continuing revolution in American politics, it was quite clear that the fundamental political trends within the nation still responded more to words than to realities. The issue of slavery in the territories had not only given birth to the Republican Party, it had also split the Democratic Party into Northern and Southern factions and prompted Northeastern and border state conservatives to launch the Constitutional Union Party to bind together the dividing nation. But if through the six confused and strenuous years that followed the Kansas-Nebraska Act the question of slavery expansion underlay all sectional politics, the issue in 1860 lacked any clear meaning for the American people. Kansas had made it clear that the territories would be free through the functioning of popular sovereignty alone, and that Stephen A. Douglas was fundamentally correct when he said that the Republican Party was not essential to keeping the territories free. It was equally certain that those Southerners who demanded equality in the territories could expect no greater support from the vast majority of Northern Democrats than they could from Republicans. The certainty that slavery would not expand removed the one issue that supposedly divided Republicans from Democrats and reduced the campaign to intellectual chaos. So complex and obscure were the attitudes of the various political factions with regard to slavery and the basic economic questions before the country—tariff, homesteads, internal improvements, and a transcontinental railroad—that no clear mandate could possibly emerge from the election.

II

Republicans launched their campaign with the assurance of victory. Sectional and half-developed as their party was, its improving chances appeared complete with the nomination of Lincoln. Four years earlier it had carried most of the North, losing only New Jersey, Pennsylvania, Indiana, Illinois, and California. It was obvious that the events of James Buchanan's administration had created Republican votes, especially the Dred Scott decision, the Panic of 1857, and the struggle over the Kansas Lecompton Constitution. In the elections of 1858 the Republican Party had won control of the House of Representatives. Thereafter the formula for victory in 1860 was simple. The party need only hold the states won by John C. Fremont in 1856 and add two of the large states Fremont had lost. This requirement established the minimum standards of availability for any Republican candidate. As Fitz-Henry Warren had said, "I am for the man who can carry Pennsylvania, New Jersey, and Indiana, with this reservation, that I will not go into cemetery or catacomb; the candidate must be alive, and able to walk, at least from parlor to dining room." At the Chicago convention the delegates from Indiana, Illinois, and Pennsylvania especially blocked the nomination of William H. Seward and supported the nomination of Lincoln as the man best qualified to carry the doubtful states.

Lincoln's selection involved one danger. Seward considered himself entitled to the nomination and confidently expected to receive it. Moreover, he and his political manager, Thurlow Weed, controlled the party in New York, a state whose electoral votes were essential for victory in November. If Seward refused to support the nominee, New York might fall to the opposition. Lincoln's convention managers, to prevent that, spent the last hour of the convention assuring Seward that he was already so distinguished that being president would add nothing to his reputation. They invited Weed to see the sights of Illinois, including the Republican choice. Seward, on hearing of Lincoln's nomination, accused Weed of selling him out. Weed replied simply that he had been outmaneuvered and outbargained.

On Friday evening, May 18, Chicago Republicans celebrated the nomination of Illinois' favorite son. They had contributed to his cause by packing the convention hall and shouting approval of Lincoln at the crucial moments during the balloting. Following the decisive third ballot, crowds formed processions and carried rails through the streets, acting out a brilliant piece of political symbolism thought up by a friend several weeks earlier. As the "rail splitter," Lincoln gained a magic nickname comparable to those employed by earlier presidential winners—Old Hickory, Old Tippecanoe, and Old Rough and Ready. One local Republican newspaper secured four rails reputedly split by Lincoln himself. Two of these were displayed outside the door of the establishment; two were festooned with candles and hung up inside.

Chicago's celebration that night was noisy and enthusiastic. "Torrents of liquor," wrote one reporter, "were poured down the hoarse throats of the multitude." Atop a leading hotel a cannon boomed out a hundred salutes, its crashes answered by others in various parts of the city. A boisterous rally at the Wigwam heard dispatches from New York, Philadelphia, and other cities declaring that ratification meetings were in progress throughout the country. Numerous buildings were lit up by placing lights in every window—a device of jubilee known as an "illumination." Bonfires blazed on corners, and skyrockets streaked across the night sky. Organized and uniformed

Republican marchers, known as Wide-Awakes, paraded about all evening, wearing gleaming oilcloth capes and carrying kerosene torches on their shoulders. They encouraged the crowds to follow them, armed with rails or anything resembling rails. At strategic points the paraders halted and released what a reporter described as "soul-inspiring cheers and exclamations of victory. . . . Babel had come again," he continued, "the Democratic Jericho shook at the shouts and blowing of trumpets and holding of torches in the left hands of Republican Gideons." Steamboat, train, and factory whistles rent the night air, and church bells chimed in to pay homage to Lincoln and his party.

One newsman who left Chicago late Friday on the crowded night train recorded his experience:

I never before saw a company of persons so prostrated by continued excitement. The Lincoln men were not able to respond to the cheers which went up along the road for "Old Abe." They had not only done their duty in that respect, but exhausted their capacity. At every station where there was a village, until after two o'clock, there were tar barrels burning, drums beating, boys carrying rails; and guns, great and small, banging away. The weary passengers were allowed no rest, but plagued by the thundering jar of cannon, the clamor of drums, the glare of bonfires, and the whooping of the boys, who were delighted with the idea of a candidate for the Presidency, who thirty years ago split rails on the Sangamon River—classic stream now and forevermore—and whose neighbors named him "honest."

Throughout Republican Illinois the scenes of Chicago were repeated in miniature. At Springfield, wrote one reporter, "there was a general firing of guns, shaking of hands, ringing of bells, harras and shouts that set the whole town in an uproar." At the statehouse a ratification meeting greeted a parade of speakers with "deafening cheers." Then behind a band the throng marched to the nominee's house a few blocks away. They cheered until Lincoln appeared. He told the crowd that he would not make a speech but would gladly invite all present inside were the house large enough to hold them. "We will," someone shouted, "give you a larger house on the fourth of next March." Lincoln retreated inside and many of his congratulators trooped in behind him.

On Saturday, May 19, Springfield Republicans were out in force to welcome the committee of notification from the Republican national convention. The special train from Chicago, packed with celebrating Republicans, was met at the depot by the Springfield Lincoln Club and, noted one observer, "a very large concourse of citizens who escorted them through the principal streets to the Chenery House . . . while the cannons fired, bonfires blazed, and rockets and other fireworks were sent up from various parts of the city, many houses upon the square being brilliantly illuminated. The streets meanwhile were crowded and the greatest enthusiasm prevailed." When the committee departed to carry out its business with Lincoln, the procession repaired to the statehouse for a rally.

Lincoln, receiving the official committee, headed by George Ashmun of Massachusetts, thanked them for the high honor done him and said that he would soon respond in writing to their invitation that he run for the presidency on the party platform. Then he shook hands with each committee member and offered them refreshments.

Mrs. Lincoln had arranged to serve hard liquor, but her husband vetoed that. He gave them ice water. Four days later Lincoln penned his acceptance of the nomination and the platform. "The declaration of principles and sentiments, which accompanies your letter," he wrote to Ashmun, "meets my approval; and it shall be my care not to violate, or disregard it, in any part."

III

Lincoln announced early that he would take no active part in the campaign. This decision followed the customary procedure of the time, but it suited his needs particularly well. Lincoln had no intention of committing himself further on any question before the nation. His debates with Douglas had already been printed in book form as a campaign document. Those who sought his views were referred to the speeches and to the Republican platform. This was not always a satisfactory response. The issue of slavery extension was largely out of date and other public questions would require some disposition by the next administration. But Lincoln's reply of October 29 to George D. Prentice, editor of the Louisville *Journal*, was typical of his attitude:

Your suggestion that I, in a certain event, shall write a letter, setting forth my conservative views and intentions, is certainly a very worthy one. But would it do any good? If I were to labor a month, I could not express my conservative views and intentions more clearly and strongly, than they are expressed in our platform, and in my many speeches already in print, and before the public. . . . If I do finally abstain, it will be because of apprehension that it would do harm. For the good men of the South—and I regard the majority of them as such—I have no objection to repeat seventy and seven times. But I have *bad* men also to deal with, both North and South—men who are eager for something new upon which to base new misrepresentations—men who would like to frighten me, or, at least, to fix upon me the character of timidity and cowardice. They would seize upon almost any letter I could write, as being an *"awful coming down."* I intend keeping my eye upon these gentlemen, and to not unnecessarily put any weapon in their hands.

This policy of silence saved Lincoln both exertion and embarrassment, and gave him the leisure to submerge himself completely in the Republican campaign from the privacy of his home. He remained in Springfield, stopped practicing law, read a flood of incoming mail, employed a personal secretary, John G. Nicolay, to assist him in handling it, talked to his numerous callers, and began going to church occasionally. Through letters and personal reports of leading politicians, he followed the progress of his opponents. In his correspondence with Republican National Chairman Edwin D. Morgan of New York and National Secretary George G. Fogg of New Hampshire he both contributed and sought advice. In one letter of the last day of October, Lincoln assured Fogg that he would not break his silence until after the election: "Allow me to beg that you will not live in much apprehension of my precipitating a letter upon the public."

Lincoln was hardly a national figure at the time of his nomination. Only two members of the notification committee had ever seen him before their arrival in Springfield. Even among party spokesmen there was some question about his name, and his letter of acceptance was almost released to the press over the name "Abram." So widely was this version of his name being used that Lincoln wrote to Ashmun on June 4: "It seems as if the question whether my first name is 'Abraham' or 'Abram' will never be settled. It is *'Abraham'* and if the letter of acceptance is not yet in print, you may, if you think fit, have my signature thereto printed *'Abraham Lincoln.'* Exercise your own judgment about this."

Republican managers acted with vigor to make the candidate known. They sent a stream of reporters, photographers, artists, and biographers to see him. Campaign biographies were hastily thrown together and issued at a minimum price, often underwritten and distributed by party organizations. Some were remarkably inaccurate, and Lincoln took the trouble in June to write a long autobiography for John L. Scripps, senior editor of the Chicago *Press & Tribune,* who was at work on his life.

With Lincoln concerned only with the general progress of the campaign, the burden of organization and publicity fell to others. From Washington campaign documents poured across the North, and with them instructions for their distribution. State central committees organized Republican clubs at the precinct level in every Northern state. In the tasks of registering voters, collecting funds, and distributing campaign literature, local Republican leaders had the advantage of a prospective victory. Crossroads politicians, anticipating a harvest of Republican loaves and fishes, hastened to join the cause. The Republican press reported regularly that some Democratic leader had decided that he had supported Douglas as long as any honest man ought to and had taken the stump for Lincoln.

To arouse enthusiasm at the endless rallies, the Republicans made much of their marching clubs, the Wide-Awakes. This movement began by accident in Hartford, Connecticut, in the spring of 1860. By convention time Chicago had organized a second company. During June and July scores of towns formed their own marching clubs, and by September almost every Northern town that was not completely Democratic boasted its own organization. The wigwam symbol was another favorite, and in every principal city a replica was erected to hold Republican meetings. Lincoln's own homely virtues and humble background added to the Republican pageantry. The theme of Lincoln the "rail splitter" gave the campaign much of the atmosphere of the "log cabin" and "hard cider" campaign of 1840. One Republican campaigner recalled that "governors, senators, and members of Congress of both parties took the stump, and for the last two months business was almost suspended, the people hastening to and fro to hear stirring speeches and to march in mile-long processions. It was a general political intoxication; the Republicans, however, everywhere surpassed their opponents in earnestness and enthusiasm." Fortunately for Republican planners, sufficient funds flowed into the party treasury to underwrite the extravagance of the campaign. But the emphasis on entertainment eliminated much serious discussion of issues.

Republican gaiety reflected the party's confidence, and that confidence, in turn, destroyed much of the campaign's anticipated excitement. The New York *World* termed it the tamest presidential contest since 1820. The New York *Evening Post* referred to its calm and quiet, and Greeley of the New York *Tribune* regarded it as far less exciting than the campaign of 1856. The reason lay partially in the comparative absence of vulnerable personalities, partially in the conviction that the Democratic Party, split as it was, simply could not win. Rufus King, editor of the Milwaukee *Sentinel,* feared that the Republican assurance of victory would become so strong that it might actually undermine the party organization. By August even Lincoln was convinced that he would sweep the entire North. On August 4 he wrote to Simeon Francis, a former resident of Springfield then residing in Oregon: "I hesitate to say it, but it really appears now, as if the success of the Republican ticket is inevitable. We have no reason to doubt any of the states which voted for Fremont. Add to these, Minnesota, Pennsylvania, and New Jersey, and the thing is done. Minnesota is as sure as such a thing can be; while the Democracy are so divided between Douglas and Breckenridge in Penn. & N.J. that they are scarcely less sure. Our friends are also confident in Indiana and Illinois. I should expect the same division would give us a fair chance in Oregon. Write me what you think on that point."

During the weeks which followed, Lincoln urged the national party organization to concentrate on Pennsylvania and Indiana, firmly convinced that Republican victories there in the October elections would assure a final party victory in Illinois as well.

IV

Lincoln's chief task—and that of his party—was that of convincing the North that its interest in free soil was safe only in Republican hands. He recognized this necessity in his Cooper Union address of February, 1860. With his customary mental agility he attempted to establish a clear distinction between the Republican Party and the Douglas Democrats on the question of slavery expansion. Without accepting a strong moral stand against slavery, he warned, no party could prevent the encroachment of the slave power on the North and its free institutions, for it was the *wrongness* of slavery that dictated the North's determination to prevent its expansion. "If it is right," he said of slavery, "we cannot justly object to its nationality—its universality; if it is wrong, they [the South] cannot justly insist on its extension—its enlargement. . . . Their thinking is right, and our thinking is wrong, is the precise point upon which depends the whole controversy." Only by calling slavery wrong—something which Douglas refused to do, ran Lincoln's argument, could the North even rationalize its effort to contain slavery.

For Lincoln, then, Northern security lay not in its superior numbers, but in its moral rectitude, for only those who admitted their hatred for slavery possessed the right to oppose its expansion. Douglas and those Northern Democrats who sought a middle ground between right and wrong, who insisted on maintaining an attitude of "don't care" on the issue of slavery, he warned, would eventually succumb to the pressure of Southern expansionists. By such reasoning Douglas was, at best, a poor risk.

Throughout the summer and autumn of 1860 Republican editors published variations on this theme. To the *Illinois State Journal* the contest in the North was primarily one between Lincoln and Douglas, between "conservative Republicanism . . . and fire-eating, slavery-extending Democracy." The entire Republican campaign against the Little Giant continued to partake of the flavor of a crusade against evil. As Caleb Cushing observed, "The political stock in trade of the Republican Party is the assumption, in some of them, perhaps, the stupid mental delusion, that whatever view they take of the measures of government is the only moral side of public questions."

Douglas rendered the task of his enemies easy, for his obligations to the South as leader of a national party had forced him on many occasions to uphold the legality of the Dred Scott decision. At New Orleans, in December, 1858, he had assured the South: "I, in common with the Democracy of Illinois, accept the decision of the Supreme Court. . . . Whatever limitation, the Constitution, as expounded by the Courts, imposes on the authority of a Territorial Legislature, we cheerfully recognize and respect in conformity with that decision. Slaves are recognized as property. . . . Hence, the owner of slaves—the same as the owner of any other species of property—has a right to remove to a Territory, and carry his property with him." By pinning Douglas to the Dred Scott decision through his own repeated statements, Republican editors could deny that there was any doctrine of popular sovereignty, and if it did exist somewhere, Douglas was not its proponent. That Douglas had frequently modified his acceptance of the Dred Scott decision with such a vigorous defense of popular sovereignty that his doctrine actually disrupted the national Democratic Party was conveniently overlooked.

When Republican editors recalled Douglas' defense of popular sovereignty, it was to accuse him of harboring two views toward slavery expansion to satisfy his supporters in both the North and the South. Never had American politics, charged the Detroit *Daily Advertiser* in August, 1860, developed "so perfect and matchless a specimen of the demagogue, as Stephen A. Douglas had proved himself to be by his career since he devised the scheme of riding into the Presidency upon the whirlwind of popular excitement, as he foresaw the repeal of the Missouri Compromise would create." Douglas, added the editor, was the perfect "doughface." It was not that he was afraid of the slave power or a defender of slavery, but that he represented that class of Democrats who asserted that they were "as much opposed to slavery as anybody" but who, in the interest of party harmony, never scrupled to sustain every measure demanded by the South.

To his Republican enemies, Douglas left nothing to choose (except the method) between his program for slavery extension and that of Breckinridge, leader of the Southern Democrats. They professed to prefer the Breckinridge platform since it was more straightforward and honest. "While Douglas attempts to *cheat* the people into the support of slavery by every conceivable fraud and misrepresentation," wrote one editor, "the friends of Breckinridge walk squarely up to the mark like bold men." The Milwaukee *Sentinel* summarized the Republican case on August 15 when it insisted that there was no visible distinction between Northern and Southern Democrats. It was because the national Democratic Party continued to force the issue of slavery extension upon the nation, continued the writer, that the Republican Party "rises again against it, saying that the bounds of slavery must be set or else there will be no end to slavery agitation. Let slavery remain a local institution . . . but let it not go out, either through squatter sovereignty or its

BRECKINRIDGE AND LANE improvisation, to become a national institution."

Such arguments permitted Republican leaders to extract whatever political advantage still remained in the threadbare issue of nonextension of slavery. Whether they convinced many Americans that slavery would expand under a Democratic hegemony is doubtful, but they assisted the Republican Party in sustaining its claims to superior morality.

Some Republican orators raised the issue of freedom. Charles Sumner, after an absence of several years, returned in 1860 to his position of leadership in the Republican Party. His peculiar brand of Republicanism was well calculated to combat the conservative views of Douglas and to prevent any defection of Republicans to the Democratic Party in the interest of national unity. His pronouncements of a "new order" were designed to strike terror into the hearts of Southerners. Without being specific as to means, he suggested that a Republican victory might somehow bring Northern power to bear on the institution of slavery. His bitter attacks on the South reduced to pure hypocrisy the protestations of Lincoln and other conservative Republicans that that section had nothing to fear. Yet those party members who believed Sumner wrong could not attack him without weakening the entire Republican organization, for much of the Republican strength hinged on its righteous opposition to slavery. The enthusiasm of Sumner's huge audiences revealed the extent of antislavery sentiment in the North and with it the hard core of Republican power. Eventually the national Republican committee published and distributed his speeches, especially in rural New England, where Sumner enjoyed his greatest popularity.

Seward, like Sumner, leveled his electioneering blasts at slavery itself. He assured a Boston audience that Lincoln was "a soldier on the side of freedom in the irrepressible conflict between freedom and slavery." From the balcony of Zach Chandler's mansion in Detroit, Seward addressed a throng of Wide-Awakes, "To-day the young men of the United States are for the first time on the side of freedom and against slavery." At St. Paul in October, Seward again interpreted the Republican campaign as a successful assault on the institution of slavery. "Slavery today is, for the first time," he told the North, "not only powerless, but without influence in the American Republic. The seried ranks of party after party, which rallied under it to sustain and support it, are broken and dissolved under the pressure of the march—the great and powerful march—of the American people, determined to restore freedom to its original and just position in the Government."

Carl Schurz, the noted spokesman of Republicanism among German-Americans, toured the Midwest in a special party appeal to German-speaking voters. His most widely quoted speech of the campaign, delivered at St. Louis on August 1, repeated the warning that slavery could not survive a Republican victory. "The slave power is impelled by the irresistible power of necessity," he said. "It cannot exist unless it rules, and it cannot rule unless it keeps down its opponents." Viewing slavery as a simple question of morality, he urged his Missouri hearers to dispense with the institution, for no political or constitutional device could sustain it. "Look around you," he told them, "and see how lonesome you are in this wide world of ours. . . . You cannot make an attempt to keep pace with the general progress of mankind, without plotting against yourselves. Every steam whistle, every puffing locomotive is sounding the shriek of liberty in your ears. From the noblest instincts of our hearts down to sordid greediness of gain, every impulse of human nature is engaged in this universal conspiracy." Slavery was doomed, not by Northern sentiment, but by the progress of the Modern World.

At best the Republican position on slavery was ambiguous, its threat to the South uncertain and undefined. Yet the party's preoccupation with the issue of freedom was eminently satisfactory to even the most ardent antislavery groups of the North. The American Anti-Slavery Society, in its *Annual Report* for 1860, admitted that it had expected a greater reliance on principle in the Republican program. "Still," the report continued, "it would be an injustice to the party not to say, that all through the campaign its presses and its speakers uttered many noble sentiments, exposed, with many words of earnest reprobation, the folly and wrong of slavery; and, with unanswerable arguments, from which they only drew modest inferences that it ought to be allowed to spread no further, proved really that it ought not to be tolerated anywhere."

V

Douglas carried the burden of undoing the political trends of the times. If Lincoln's only hope for success lay in the continued alienation of Northern voters from their political affiliations with the South, Douglas required nothing less than a reunification of the Democratic Party. Yet the hostility between the two major Democratic factions tended to increase rather than diminish as the campaign progressed. Some powerful Democratic editors, even in the North, accused Douglas of breaking up the party. The Albany *Atlas & Argus* declared that if Douglas had stepped aside the party could have agreed on another candidate. Such critics denied that Douglas, who had not received a two-thirds vote of a regular party convention, was even a legitimate nominee. Republican editors capitalized on such Democratic charges. One called him the "bogus candidate."

Douglas, informed by his national chairman, August Belmont of New York, that Democratic contributions would be meager, decided to overcome the deficit by defying precedent and personally stumping the country. He hoped that a hard and vigorous campaign, with repeated speaking engagements, might offset Lincoln's advantage. During July and August he toured New England, allegedly to visit his birthplace in Vermont, but actually to address audiences everywhere and confer with party leaders. He returned to Washington to consider his next move. Then he turned to the South, visiting Virginia and North Carolina. There in Breckinridge territory he faced without evasion the question of secession. He would hang, he declared at Raleigh, every man higher than Haman who would resist the execution of any provision of the Constitution. Finding himself hemmed in by the extremes, Douglas struck out with equal vigor in both directions. During his tour of Maryland, he announced that he was prepared to bury Southern disunionists and Northern abolitionists in the same grave. In

September he declared before a New York audience: "I wish to God we had an Old Hickory now alive in order that he might hang Northern and Southern traitors on the same gallows."

Republican editorials ridiculed Douglas' travels about the country. One called him the "wandering demagogue." To the St. Louis *Democrat* his personal campaigning marked the full degeneracy of the Democratic Party. "Hitherto such candidates have maintained a discreet silence . . . to the close of the canvass," continued the rebuke, "[but] Mr. Douglas, under one pretext or another, is vagabondizing all over New England and New York, and availing himself of every halt at a railroad depot to make a stump speech, in which he vilifies the Republican party almost as much as the party which is headed by Breckinridge." Contrasting Douglas' "naked demagoguery" with the "reserved and modest bearing" of Lincoln, the writer concluded: "Since the day of his nomination, Mr. Lincoln has never left Springfield, nor spoken, nor written a word for the public, with the exception of his brief note of acceptance."

Everywhere in the North Douglas found the tide running hard against him. He was forced to carry the burden of the alleged corruption of the Buchanan administration. The Congressional committee, charged with the investigation of several government departments, made available its report in the summer of 1860. An abridgment was published by the Republican Congressional campaign committee and distributed widely across the nation while Republican editors informed their readers of its contents. This strengthened the Republican argument that it was time for a change.

Many Democrats, convinced that Douglas could not win, continued to bolt to the Republican side. Nor could Bell make any compensating inroads among the old-line Whigs. The choice of Lincoln, a lifelong supporter of Henry Clay, prevented any conservative revolt from Republican ranks. In the key state of Pennsylvania, Republicans attacked Douglas effectively for his low tariff views. Lincoln aided his party's cause by writing privately to James E. Harvey, correspondent of the Philadelphia *North American:* "In 1844 I was on the Clay electoral ticket in this State [Illinois] and, to the best of my ability, sustained, together, the tariff of 1842 and the tariff plank of the Clay platform. This could be proven by hundreds—perhaps thousands—of living witnesses." One Pennsylvania Democrat urged the Southerners in the Senate to sacrifice their principles a little and pass a high tariff to save the Democratic Party in the Keystone State. In the Northwest, especially in Indiana and Illinois, Douglas was powerless to counter the Republican campaign promises of internal improvements and a transcontinental railroad, issues which had long excited the enthusiasm of the region.

In October, while visiting Iowa, Douglas received the news that the Republicans had carried the state elections in Pennsylvania, Ohio, and Indiana. He admitted finally that Lincoln would be the next president, adding, "We must try to save the Union. I will go South." He hurried into the deep South to battle his enemies there, but few Southerners would support the author of the Freeport Doctrine. During the closing weeks of the campaign, when the drift in the North brought the warning of impending disaster, Democratic politicians, North and

South, proposed that all candidates opposed to Lincoln withdraw and agree on a fusion leader, perhaps Horatio Seymour of New York. Douglas refused, declaring that his followers would vote for Lincoln rather than any other Democratic candidate. Eventually to save New York from a Republican victory, the anti-Lincoln forces succeeded in forming a "fusion" electoral ticket, but the move came too late. On November 1, Chairman Morgan predicted a Republican majority in New York of not less than 40,000.

VI

Southern politicians and editors reduced their campaign to a contest between Breckinridge and Bell, for these two candidates represented the fundamental struggle between those who favored and those who opposed the Southern movement for independence. As the Nashville *Banner* explained in August:

Here in the South it is a waste of labor to fight Republicanism, or its representative, Abe Lincoln. There is but one opinion here in regard to that party—and that is that it is sectional, aggressive upon the South, and founded upon an idea to resist the triumph of which every Southern man should be willing to sacrifice all other political issues, and make common enemy. We have not, therefore, in this canvass, devoted much of our space to an exposition of the position and purpose of the Republican party, preferring rather to leave that duty to our gallant Northern Union men, who have the enemy in their midst, while we, meanwhile, turn our attention to the sectional spirit which infests the Southern states, and which, under the lead of such restless and dangerous spirits as Yancey, Keitt, Rhett, Spratt, and their fellow disunionists threaten, equally with Republicanism North, to prove a wedge to split the Union in twain.

Rhett and his band of Southern patriots were determined to give the crisis of 1860 an air of finality. What played into their hands were the Republican efforts to define the central issue of the campaign as the struggle between freedom and slavery. Perhaps much of the Republican argumentation was meant for the North—to draw a clear moral distinction between Republicanism and Douglas' doctrine of popular sovereignty. But the speeches of men like Sumner and Seward were prominently displayed in the Southern press and forced many of the doubtful to the conclusion that the Republican Party represented an assault on the Constitutional rights of the Southern people. If victorious, that party would plunder the South in the interest of Northern profits. The only real issue of the campaign was, therefore, whether Southern "social security or financial prosperity" could withstand "Northern Republican license." Recounting the progressive isolation of the South during twenty years of sectional conflict, the Charleston *Mercury* concluded in June, 1860: "The Northern people have forced upon us the conviction, reluctantly and slowly attained, that no submission on our part can win their forebearance, and no rights escape their violation, and that our safety rests in ourselves. . . ."

As the legislatures of South Carolina, Alabama, and Mississippi made preliminary moves toward secession, the Northern Democratic and Constitutional Union presses attempted to inform the North of Southern intentions. It was essential, declared one Douglas paper, that the people of the North should recognize the peril from "the unanimous tone of the Southern press; the plain business-like statements . . . showing the utter impossibility of the South's remaining in the Union should our National Government pass under the control of Black Republican fanatics." Republicans dismissed the threats of disunion as little but Democratic electioneering. It was the final, desperate effort of a divided party "to bully the people out of their choice." The threat had been repeated so often that few Northerners would react any longer. "Who's afraid?" Seward asked a Minnesota audience, then answered, "Nobody's afraid; nobody can be bought."

What undermined the impact of secessionist sentiment on the North in 1860 was the continued strength of Southern Unionism. It was this opinion, said Republicans, that measured the true mood of the South. Throughout Georgia and the border states especially leading members of the press carried the war against the radicals. Their appeal to the South was anchored to political realism. Nowhere, they pointed out, had the South suffered any loss or humiliation from Northern fanaticism. Nor would it in the future, for there was no Republican program for achieving what Republican orators preached. If the election of Lincoln would be a catastrophe for true patriots, North and South, it could furnish, said the New Orleans *Bee,* "no possible excuse for hasty and precipitate action on the part of the South." Southern security lay not in independence, but in Northern allies in Congress, in the Constitution and the courts. Outside the Union, moreover, the South would lose its Northern markets and sources of supply and capital. Secession would simply draw the business and wealth of the South into the border states along the Ohio and Mississippi rivers. "Charleston," warned the Memphis *Appeal* in October, "instead of becoming the great political and commercial capital of a Southern Confederacy, would dwindle into utter insignificance, while Memphis would grow apace in wealth and population. . . ."

Finally, Southern moderates assured the South that it had no Constitutional right to secession. Said the Augusta *Chronicle and Sentinel* in accusing disunionists of harboring revolutionary doctrine,

The Constitutional right of peaceable secession is the most senseless of things ever discussed by wise men. Everybody knows that while a State, and indeed every Citizen of that State, may hold the opinion that such State has the right to secede when it pleases, it being the sole judge for itself of infraction of the Compact of Union, yet if the other states happen to think that there has been no violation of the organic law, except by the attempt of secession, and choose to attempt coercion, it brings the seceding party face to face with revolution, and to the final test of *all right, might*. The right of secession is not worth a fig, as long as others choose to test that right by force.

Clearly the South, if it would leave the Union, would be forced to fight its way out.

VII

Lincoln carried the entire North in November, yet he was a minority president, polling scarcely 40 per cent of the total votes cast. Both the Republican and Democratic parties increased their voting percentages over 1856, largely at the expense of the Americans. Lincoln increased the Republican vote by 120,000 in Pennsylvania, by 30,000 in New Jersey, by 45,000 in Indiana, and by 76,000 in Illinois. His gains were made largely in rural districts. In the Northwest, the lake region demonstrated its political dominance, its heavy concentration of German and Yankee voters tipping the balance for the Republican Party.

Douglas ran a strong second to Lincoln in the popular vote, 1,376,957 to 1,866,452, but carried only one state—Missouri. The Constitutional Union Party, having adopted no platform on slavery, had a wide appeal in the Unionist border states, carrying Virginia, Kentucky, and Tennessee. Even in the deep South where Breckinridge triumphed, the Constitutional Union forces enjoyed an advantage over Douglas, for they were not bound by any rigid commitments to precise sectional views and could agree with the Breckinridge Democrats on almost every issue and promise the continuation of the Union besides.

Lincoln's victory, however, did not result from the Democratic schism. To this he owed only 15 of his 180 electoral votes. Had all his opponents agreed on one candidate, he would still have carried all his states but California and Oregon, leaving him 21 electoral votes above a majority. His victory resulted from the fact that he carried, often by narrow margins, those heavily populated regions of the United States where political and economic power had been accumulating for a decade. Lincoln's election demonstrated beyond every doubt what the politics of the fifties had often denied—that the South had been reduced to a minority position.

Lincoln's triumph merely intensified the divisions within the South already evident throughout the campaign. Much of the Southern press interpreted the election as a clear threat to the South and its institutions. The New Orleans *Crescent* responded immediately with a shrill warning: "The Northern people, in electing Mr. Lincoln, have perpetrated a deliberate, cold blooded insult and outrage upon the people of the slaveholding states. Further than this, the election has been conducted by their orators and presses, upon a platform of inextinguishable hatred, which if carried out, would leave no right or property or franchise, or interest of the South worth maintaining, to our people."

In many areas of the South editors found their people despondent at the news of Lincoln's election. "We read the result on the face of every citizen upon the street," observed one troubled New Orleans editor. In similar language the Memphis *Appeal* recorded the reaction in its city: "The confirmation of this sad intelligence yesterday cast a gloom of dispair about the city, which was plainly depicted upon the countenances of all parties. . . . In the intensity of their regret—in the profoundness of their gloom—in the danger of their surroundings—*party* has been forgotten in the thoughts of COUNTRY!" Fortunately, added one Louisiana editor, neither the Supreme Court nor the Congress had come under the control of fanatics. The South was safe for two more years. But the past made it clear that the future carried no hope. "Under the circumstance," continued his editorial, "it is not wonderful that a deep and profound excitement pervades the South. . . . Last Tuesday there was no disunion party in New Orleans. To-day we would not care about trying the issue at the ballot-box. The wanton conduct of the Northern people has produced the natural result in the South." Party distinctions in the South were fast disintegrating.

Southern Unionists rushed into the fray, determined to prevent the formation of a monolithic South which might seek its security outside the Republic. They accused the extremists of attempting to place the Southern populace in a position from which it could not retreat with honor, and thus force a showdown in the sectional conflict. They admitted that the party of Lincoln was hostile to the spirit of the Constitution and could not be ignored. But they sought to draw a clear distinction between Republican words and Republican power. They accused Southern radicals of overestimating the damage that a Northern party and Northern attitudes could inflict on the South. "Sensitive and chivalric," ran the New Orleans *Picayune*'s judgment of Southerners, "they see little difference between the utterances of a warm political contest, and the practical direction of legislation and the direct use of executive power to accomplish all of the revolution in the policy of the Government foreshadowed by the factious apostles of Republicanism." In short, ran the Unionist argument, the Republican threat had never been more than verbal.

Moderates assured the self-appointed spokesmen of Southern patriotism that they would be the first to resist any open, undisguised violation of Southern rights. They were not less true to the South, they insisted, because they were also true to the Union. They were no less mindful of the challenge of the North because they preferred to meet it as citizens of the United States. The Baltimore *American* conceded the South the right to condemn Republican principles, but added that "we do insist upon maintaining our position of equality in the Union, and watching over our rights from the Ohio to the great lakes. . . ." Similarly the Lexington *Statesman* reminded the South that the people of Kentucky would not submit to wrong or dishonor, but added emphatically, "they do not believe the time has come for revolution, and will yet cling to the Union with the devotion of the sons of '76." Should the Republican threat to Southern rights ever become actual, said the moderates, they would be the first to react, for they were as cognizant of Southern interests as were their more vociferous Southern opponents.

Fundamentally Southern Unionists emphasized the theme that the South was not powerless to defend itself in a Republican-dominated nation. Thus they could discover no advantage for the South in the abandonment of its position in the Union. With the North established as a foreign country, it was quite certain that there would be fewer fugitive slaves returned in the future than in the past. If the South had lost out in the territories, the issue had been determined long before Lincoln's election. Nor would the South improve its chances of obtaining additional slave territory by declaring its independence. Outside the Union, moreover, the South would lose much of its established security. The Louisville *Democrat* was one of many border state newspapers that challenged the view that cotton was king and that cotton would guarantee the South any unique political, economic, and diplomatic success. A Southern republic, cautioned the editor, "might have resources enough to protect itself, and get along respectably, [but] it could not present the formidable power for protection and progress that this Union presents."

In the crisis created by Lincoln's election, Northern editors took hope from the upsurge of moderation in the South. Many sought to strengthen this tendency by reassuring the South that it had nothing to fear. The Cincinnati *Gazette* reminded its readers across the Ohio that the principles of Lincoln were identical with those of Henry Clay. Both men hated slavery and regarded its extension as an unnecessary evil; both were willing to tolerate the institution where it already existed. The real enemies of the North, continued the editor in a powerful summary of the Northern conservative position, were those Northern editors and politicians who persistently misrepresented Northern sentiment. "They never make a statement," he charged on November 22, 1860,

which is not either directly or indirectly a libel upon a great and powerful body of Northern voters, composing a majority of its most intelligent, calm-thinking, and conservative citizens. These false and malicious statements are eagerly copied by Southern Democratic journals, and read by Southern people, and thus they contract the prejudices and hostile feelings toward the North, which we find so general in that section. These Northern incendiary sheets are eternally warning the South of impending ruin in case of the success of the Republican party, and that its object is to wage a war of extermination against their rights and institutions. The millions of respectable and law-abiding men [of the North] . . . constitute a party which is no more radical on the Slavery question than the old Whig party, and . . . has elected a President who stands in the footsteps of the gallant old leader of that glorious old party. . . .

Some Republicans interpreted Lincoln's election as a victory for Whiggery, not freedom. John Sherman observed: "We know very well that the great objects which those who elected Mr. Lincoln expect him to accomplish will be to secure to free labor its just right to the Territories . . . ; to protect . . . by wise revenue laws the labor of our people; to secure the public lands to actual settlers . . . ; to develop the internal resources of the country by opening new means of communication between the Atlantic and the Pacific. . . ." For some the election signified nothing more than a substitution of one administration for another—one that promised greater honesty than its predecessor but certainly posed no greater threat to Southern institutions. Believing that Lincoln would deliver the country from a reign of corruption and sectional agitation, the conservative Baltimore *Patriot* concluded: "What friend of the Union, of the nation, of the country—what man in favor of ceasing fruitless agitation and restoring peace and harmony, will not rejoice at the result?"

With each editor and politician analyzing the election in terms of his own philosophy or interests, thoughtful Americans understandably could not agree on its meaning. Both the rhetoric of the campaign and the returns themselves indicated that the dominant political tendencies in North and South were anchored firmly to sectional issues. Whether there could be any retreat to moderation and compromise by whole populations was doubtful, for the salvation of party, then as always, was the chief concern of politicians.

For a powerful minority in both sections—those who crusaded against the institution of slavery and those who answered with a determination to defend all their rights to its continuance—Northern voters had achieved a revolution in the American political and Constitutional order through the mere act of casting ballots. Obviously this could not be true, for the nation's political traditons, whether the reflection of Constitutional limitations or of the distribution of political power, were far too stable to be rent asunder by a simple, thoroughly legal presidential election. In short, too much power had been assigned to words, but words carry both hopes and fears, and once the concepts which they carry become embedded in basic human emotions and reflexes, men often find it difficult to distinguish between their ambitions and their requirements, between their fears and their vulnerability. Yet unless those responsible for the country's welfare could make such distinctions better in the future than they had in the past, the Union's days were numbered.

V

The Fatal Predicament

"In any civil war the question of war guilt is of the deepest importance." A feeling of self-righteousness and a firm belief in the depravity of the enemy builds morale in war days and helps to justify the heavy cost when the struggle is ended. Thereafter the victor may glory in the triumph of truth and righteousness; the defeated may find consolation in having fought nobly for a noble cause.

Since both sides invariably call legality, morality, and tradition to their assistance, the historian, even a hundred years later, still feels the pressure of emotions generated. The debate seemingly never ends, and that calm objectivity which permits a feeling of sorrow for a whole people who drifted into a situation where only bloodshed would serve is long in coming. Yet when a united nation expects the descendants of both victor and vanquished to join in a centennial celebration of such a civil war, about the only permanent good that can be hoped for is the hastening of such an attitude. Little of national value can result from the re-enactment of battles as romantic episodes devoid of all the horrors of death and destruction, or from the recounting of events cast in the pattern of good men facing bad men and truth opposing error. Nations do not learn wisdom from such things.

It is for this reason that the historian might better stress the blindness, the blundering, and the helplessness of men on the eve of the American Civil War, and deal with it as a national tragedy, not as a romantic museum piece—as something to regret and to gain a lesson from, not as something to glorify.

If we must have a simple statement of how this Civil War came about, we need only to remember that a sectional controversy changed from words to action when eleven Southern states, one by one, attempted to withdraw from the Union, and the administration in Washington refused to allow them to do so. Each side then revealed the depths of its feelings and the uncompromisable character of their disagreement by a willingness to go to war in defense of the position taken. That turned the struggle into one of preserving the Union on the one side, and of defending the legal rights of a state on the other. It simplified the complex differences which, for decades, had been driving the sections apart and reduced them to a conflict of principles. Each position had value in stirring men to fight for "the right" and in throwing war guilt onto the other.

But such an approach, although it served well the purposes of the moment, is of little value to the historian. Secession and Northern resistance to it were merely the final stages in a situation that had long been developing. The really fundamental questions as to why the Southern states insisted on leaving the Union, and why the Northern states would not permit them to go, are left unanswered. It does not tell why men who had so recently united in forming "a more perfect union" now thought of themselves as two distinct peoples, hating each other with "a Carthaginian hatred." Few men in either North or South could have answered those questions. Nor have the historians of succeeding years been able to do so in a satisfactory way.

II

In order to justify secession, most of the Southern states did attempt statements of grievances. These were made as much to convince their own reluctant citizens as to satisfy the outside world. They, therefore, dealt primarily with those immediate abuses and threats which would have the greatest emotional appeal. Underlying factors were largely ignored. Yet these statements did reveal the final patterns into which all differences had been cast—the symbols which covered and took the place of details.

South Carolina led off with an elaborate assertion of the Federal-compact character of the American government which permitted withdrawal when one party did not live up to its obligations. The stipulation to return fugitive slaves, they said, had been written into the Constitution, and that this compact would not have been made without it. Yet Northern states had openly refused to live up to their obligations. They had passed laws which nullified the acts of Congress, or "rendered useless any attempt to exercise them." Some states had refused to surrender to justice those who had incited servile insurrections. All of them had denounced the Southern domestic institution of slavery as sinful, and had now "united in the election of a man to the high office of President of the United States whose opinions and purposes were hostile to slavery" and to its future expansion. Public opinion "at the North" had thus "invested a great political error with the sanction of a more erroneous religious belief."

The other seceding states of the lower South followed this same line of defense. They varied their statements to fit local conditions, but stressed the threat to domestic institutions and their inability to protect themselves longer. Georgians, for example, spoke of "the feeling of insecurity" among the people who had become a permanent minority, and of the "imminent peril" of "being in the power of a majority reckless of Constitutional obligations and pledged to principles leading to our destruction." They, too, pointed as proof to the refusal to surrender fugitive slaves. Alabama saw Lincoln's election as the triumph of a sectional party "hostile to the domestic institutions and to the peace and security" of the state. It was "a political wrong of so insulting and menacing a character as to justify secession." Mississippi declared herself to be "so identified with the institution of slavery" that she had no choice left but submission to the mandates of abolition, or a dissolution of the Union. Hostility to slavery had trampled underfoot "the original equality of the South," denied her the right of expansion, nullified the Fugitive Slave Law, and destroyed the compact made by the Founding Fathers. Secession was "not a matter of choice but of necessity." Texas, somewhat more concerned with the way Southerners had been excluded from the territories, ascribed it all to a Northern desire to gain control of "the common government, to use it as a means of destroying the institutions of Texas and her sister slave-holding states." She also complained of the lack of Federal protection, of the acts against the returning of fugitives, and of the final reduction of the South "to a hopeless minority."

It is thus apparent that slavery, its protection, its expansion, and even its moral standing, had become the symbol of Northern aggression and of Southern rights. Even the reforms sometimes suggested by the conservative opposition in these states dealt almost exclusively with the protection of slavery.

The border states had additional reasons for action. The pathetic and indignant statements that came from their conventions carry a note of betrayal and of bitterness at Lincoln's call for troops to put down rebellion. They needed only to say that up until now they had remained in the Union "loyally discharging all their duties under the Constitution, in the hope that what was threatening in public affairs might yield to the united efforts of patriotic men from every part of the nation, and by these efforts such guarantees for the security of our rights might be obtained as should restore confidence, renew alienated ties, and finally reunite all the states in a common bond of fraternal union. . . ." They now found their ports blockaded, their soil threatened with invasion, and their help demanded in waging "a cruel war." They had no alternative to secession.

III

Now the interesting thing about the reasons given by the Southern states for leaving the Union in 1860 and 1861 is the almost total absence of concrete and specific cases of injury other than those relating to fugitive slaves. Emphasis is almost exclusively on such intangibles as the violation of assumed Constitutional rights, on unjust criticisms of Southern institutions, and on apprehensions of dangers yet to come. Indignation, hurt pride, and stark fear are revealed in every line. The haunting prospect of inequality, perhaps even of inferiority, is strikingly apparent.

In other words, a careful appraisal of Southern complaints offered in 1860 leaves much to be explained. There is too wide a gap between the emotional reactions and the actual damage done. Either the Southerners were not justified in taking the extreme step or, somehow, they had come to know that they stood helpless before an all-destroying force. Even in the matter of fugitive slaves the historian finds an element of uncertainty regarding the actual damage suffered. Only a very small percentage of those held in bondage ever became permanent runaways, and there is absolutely no way of knowing how many of these few crossed the Mason-Dixon Line. Information in this field is scanty, and much of it unreliable. Southerners exaggerated their losses for propaganda purposes, and abolitionists, in old age, remembered their aid to fugitives through the magnifying haze of time. At any rate, the United States Census found only .0003 per cent of all slaves to have been fugitives in 1850. Unquestionably the great majority of these never left the South. Fewer of them had run away because of Northern influence.

This figure is probably as unreliable as are others. But it does show that material losses did not disturb the South half so much as did the clearly revealed fact that neither the Constitution nor the laws of Congress could longer protect the South in its right to the return of fugitive slaves. There were limits beyond which Northern consciences would not go.

A closer look at the territorial issue is also revealing. Ever since the late 1840's the chief Southern complaints against the North had been the denial of equal access to the territories. This had brought threats of secession and had precipitated a serious national crisis in 1850. "Wilmot Proviso" and "California" had become fighting words, as had "Kansas" and "Lecompton Constitution" a few years later. Yet in the statements made in 1860, there were only vague and scattered references to the territories. Even in these, the emphasis was on the fact that the South had been denied equality and not on the loss of territory. The reasons for this were simple. There had not been, in the first place, any particular need for the expansion of slavery, and few intelligent Southerners had thought the existing territories fitted for it anyway. They had fought for a principle. Now, in 1860, it was perfectly clear that the people themselves in both California and Kansas, by the normal process of permanent settlement, had made the decision for freedom. It had not been the work of any administration, or of any one politician or any one party. Time had taken care of the issue.

In the case of Kansas, for instance, editors all over the South, by 1858, were declaring themselves "heartily tired of seeing the word Kansas" and were convinced that "the question of slavery had been settled by the parties in that territory." As one conservative Southerner wrote: "It is certainly a small matter of gain to the South to have Kansas come in with a slave Constitution, & so to remain *only* until the Legislature can convene & call a Convention that will immediately assemble and, infuriated with a slavery constitution being forced on them, will abolish slavery without reference to the interests of slave owners. . . ." "We have long looked upon the fate of Kansas as sealed," wrote a South Carolina editor, "and have been frequently amused at the strenuous efforts which Southern politicians make, not to secure the territory to the South, but to be cheated out of it according to the letter of the law." He even defended Douglas because Douglas had done only what he had to do if he were to continue in public office. "The South," he added, "is too ready to find solace for her misfortunes in abusing those who will not cut their throats to save her."

The very use of the term "misfortunes" as well as the fair understanding of Douglas' situation shows that one South Carolinian, at least, understood that both the men of the North and of the South were in a sad predicament—the victims of circumstances. Evidently, he understood that the territorial issue was only a surface expression of a more fundamental clash.

Nor is the Southern charge of a Northern conspiracy in the triumph of a sectional party very convincing. It is true, of course, that the Republican Party was a sectional party, and that it had achieved formal organization with the passage of the Kansas-Nebraska Act. Its immediate stated purpose was to resist the spread of slavery into the territories, but powerful political parties are not born on the spur of the moment. The Republican Party had been long in the making, and

Kansas was only the immediate occasion for its emergence.

The same forces which had destroyed the Whig Party, and which had brought the Liberty and the Free Soil parties into being; the same conditions which had created the notion that there was a slave power operating in political life, and that Southern policies stood across the path of progress and the realization of the material possibilities of both Northeast and Northwest—these were the real forces that created the unfounded fear that Kansas might become a slave state and that hurried forward the formation of the Republican Party. Back of this, however, lay the perfectly apparent need for a new political party representing the interests of the expanding North as an industrial society and as a land of freedom.

We are not questioning the sincerity of Northern attitudes regarding the moral weaknesses of slavery when we insist that industrial capitalism and consolidated nationalism were not compatible with Southern political dominance; we are not denying the ingrained democratic values of Northern men when we say that they also wanted tariffs, sound credit policies, river and harbor improvements, and homesteads. We are not saying that men live by bread alone when we point to the simple truth that the Republican Party was the carrier not only of men's values, but of their interests as well. As such, it had to be a sectional party, but it was not less so than Southern demands at Charleston in 1860 would have made the Democratic Party. Southerners could justly grumble against the working of fate, but they could not fairly ascribe Lincoln's election to Northern intrigue.

William A. Graham of North Carolina saw the situation clearly:

Our government is not an elected monarchy but a representative republic. High as this office [the presidency] may be supposed to exalt the man, he is at last but the servant of the people, and clothed only with powers to do good. If these powers are perverted to our injury and oppression, resistance will be made with united hearts, and with the hope of success; but who can prepare a declaration of independence, appealing to a candid world for its approbation and sympathy, upon the ground that we have been outvoted in an election, in which we took the chance of success, and a candidate has been elected, who, however obnoxious, we did not deem unworthy to compete with for votes? . . . Let us not injure a cause capable of the best defense, and admitted to be imperiled, by taking council of passion, not of wisdom.

But regardless of the soundness or the unsoundness of other Southern complaints, the attack on slavery as a sin to be confessed and abandoned at once was an entirely different matter. Slavery had been an integral part of Southern life for at least 200 years. Its people had often viewed it as a misfortune but never as a sin. Their clergy had defended it and the scriptures had been a favorite source for defense. Southerners were not ready to confess moral inferiority. So to hear a United States Senator speak of "the whole slave-holding class as a combination of ruffianism and bluster, whiskey-drinking and tobacco-chewing," and to be "held up to the gaze of an eager world as slave drivers, lost to humanity and accursed of God" was adding insult to injury.

Nor could Southerners view the sudden abandonment of slavery as so simple a matter as did the Northern reformers. The Negro slave constituted the laboring force of the plantation and the domestic servant in the home. As property, he represented millions of dollars of invested capital, and Professor Thomas R. Dew had long ago warned the section that emancipation would wreck its economy and plunge it into bankruptcy.

The social threat was even greater. The presence of three and a half million Negroes held in bondage presented, at all times, a serious race question. Agitation, even without action, was a danger. The immediate ending of all slavery controls, even for moral reasons, meant social chaos. As the Charleston *Mercury* said, the Southerner was not left to speculate in order to know "the fate of white men in a community of liberated negroes." "Where are the white non-slaveholders of Haiti," he asked, and then answered, "Slaughtered or driven out of that grand paradise of abolitionism."

Suppose the object of the Northern abolitionists then accomplished . . . a strife will arise between the white men who remain . . . and the negroes, compared to which the atrocities and crimes of ordinary wars, are peace itself. The midnight glare of the incendiary's torch will illuminate the country from one end to the other; while pillage, violence, murder, poisons and rape will fill the air with the demoniac revelry of all the passions of an ignorant, semi-barbarous race, urged to madness by the licentious teachings of our Northern brethren. A war of races—a war of extirmination—must arise, like that which took place in St. Domingo. . . . The people of the Northern states cannot, or will not, understand this state of things. . . . The doom they are ready to visit upon the poor white man of the South, they would not dare propose to the white laborers of the North.

All this, of course, had to do mainly with anticipated troubles, not always with aggressions already committed. It does, however, confirm the truth of Judah P. Benjamin's statement that it was not so much what the Republicans and abolitionists had done or might do that counted, as it was "the things they said," and the assumption of moral superiority with which they were said. Because they were "sinners," Southerners were being asked to accept a violent socioeconomic revolution by men who assumed that "the Earth belongs to the Saints and that they are the Saints of the Lord," and who would in no way be inconvenienced by the violence.

The good clergyman who offered prayer at the opening of the Mississippi convention added a deeper reason for Southern action. After jogging the Lord's memory of "the maligned and mighty agencies which many of the sister states of this great national family have employed for our annoyance, reproach and overthrow, as equals in the Confederated Union," he called attention especially to the purpose pursued "of depriving us of our just rights, and destroying in our midst the institution which Thy Providence has solemnly bound us to uphold, defend, and protect." They too had moral obligations!

IV

With Lincoln's election, the Southern states, one after the other, held their conventions and declared themselves out of the Union. They talked of "submission or secession" as an effort to escape further Northern aggression, but as a matter of cold fact they were protesting against the loss of status. Their equality as a section was gone. Economically, they had been reduced to colonial dependence. Socially, their domestic institutions, once accepted, were under condemnation throughout the Western world. Politically, they were a permanent minority.

They were right when they charged that their way of life was no longer safe in the Union. Even their Constitutional rights were no longer secure where men talked of a "higher law." They were wrong only in placing the blame too largely in the wrong place. Northerners had provided the irritations; they had flung the bitter facts into Southern faces, they had waged an unceasing war on slavery and condemned it to ultimate extinction; but their real offense was that they had become the allies of the true culprit—*the Modern World* of Nationalism, the Industrial Revolution, and Freedom.

In this latter fact also lay the basic reasons for Northern refusal to allow the Southern states to break up the Union and to depart in peace. It was this which gave them the unwarranted feeling of self-righteousness. They themselves had not always been such ardent nationalists. There had been among them many who had been openly disloyal during both the War of 1812 and the Mexican War. These had hoped for American defeat and had talked of secession. Thirteen Northern members of Congress had signed a declaration saying that the annexation of Texas would justify a dissolution of the Union. State after state had passed their personal-liberty laws in open defiance of the Constitution and the laws of Congress, and a few had made a bonfire out of that document. The Wisconsin legislature, in 1859, had gone so far as to resolve that the Federal Government was not the final judge of the powers delegated to it.

Even in 1860, there were men in almost every North-

ern state who defended the right of secession. A Rhode
Island editor declared that "even a single state . . . may
with dignity gather her full robes of majesty about her
and leave the confederacy which has already left her."
He asserted that the "right of secession" was "the right
[of a state] to keep itself intact from encroachment or
annihilation." An Ohio editor bluntly stated that "if
South Carolina wants to go out of the Union, she has a
right to do so," and another frankly expressed the opinion
"that any state of the confederation has, or at least ought
to have, a perfect and undoubted right to withdraw from
the Union. . . ." It was "one of the 'reserved rights' of
the States." A New Hampshire editor went so far as to
say that Northern Democrats would not aid the Republicans in conquering the South. "If they have courage
to undertake the task, they will have to undertake it
alone, and when they march down to subdue the South,
they will have a fire in the rear which will not add either
to the pleasure or the success of their enterprise." In
other words, Northern love of the Union, like the Southern distrust of it, had been a growth under changing conditions. They had only recently been ready to fight for its
preservation.

There were, of course, some sound economic reasons
for opposing secession. Men of the Northwest saw a
threat to their trade. "Are these men fools?" asked Edward
Bates. "Do they flatter themselves with the foolish thought
that we of the upper Mississippi will ever submit to have
the mouth of our river held by a foreign power, whether
friend or foe? Do they not know that that is a fighting
question, and not fit to be debated?"

Other Westerners saw their section "hemmed in,

isolated, cut off from the seaboard on every side" and gradually sinking "into a pastoral state." Peaceful secession was out of the question.

Industrial and commercial centers also understood clearly that they were dependent on the nation as a whole both for markets and for raw materials in this day of mass production. As a Northern businessman said: "We cannot afford to have established on this continent the intolerable restrictions to commercial intercourse, which are fast dying out among the nations of Europe."

V

Economic interests, however, do not adequately explain Northern attitudes. A few, at first, talked of letting the erring sisters go, but when the reality of a divided nation had to be faced, a quick reaction followed. They discovered that they had become *nationalists:* that there had grown up among them a firm conviction that the United States was indivisible and that it had a manifest destiny to fulfill; that something which belonged to all Americans, North and South alike, was being threatened —an intangible, spiritual something, which gave America its meaning and in which God himself had an interest. They owed it to mankind to resist the destruction of democratic government, man's last best hope.

Such sentiments, however, needed a firm foundation on which to rest. The census gave swaggering evidence of wide material growth and of the superiority of a society where cities, factories, and commerce held sway. The North was in step with progress. It might have taken even more rapid strides had not the South opposed. But what they had accomplished was enough to silence the criticism only recently hurled at their new industrial capitalists, and to quiet the fears which machinery had stirred.

A feeling of moral superiority was also justified by the near-unanimous opposition to the further spread of slavery. Even the politician was calling slavery a relic of the Dark Ages and a blot on the national escutcheon. The contempt for the abolitionist, once almost as common, had given way to the conviction that slavery must be put on the road to ultimate extinction. The nation could not endure half free and half slave. Republicans, at least, had enlisted for the duration. They had no "olive branches" to offer the South. As one wrote:

We cannot tell Mr. Yancy that we do not believe slavery wrong, for the reverse is the profound conviction of three fourths of the whole North, all parties included. This conviction takes its birth in the best instincts of our nature and is fortified by the principles of Christianity, the chief preachers of all ages and countries, by the teachings of legal writers, by the inspirations of poetry, by the laws of civilization. The belief that slavery is wrong is as firmly settled in the minds and hearts of the people as any article of their religious creed. It would be dishonest to say that this conviction will not remain and grow stronger every day.

Nor could he truthfully say that fugitive slaves would ever be returned. Even if the personal-liberty laws should be repealed, "the sentiments, movements, tendencies, principles and moral and economic laws" would remain unchanged. The South was asking for "an impossible revolution in the moral and political convictions" of Northern men, and to say that slavery could live without such a revolution was to tell another falsehood.

"Then," he continued, "if these things are so, to

assure the secessionists that slavery shall be protected and made perpetual, and that it shall be extended and recognized as a controlling power in the Union, and that all opposition to it shall cease, would be to tell a base lie, and a very foolish lie. As well promise them that water shall run uphill and two and two shall make five."

Thus nationalism, progress, and a truer democracy had united in what was becoming a sectional crusade, a consciousness of a mission. One day it would find its battle song in a strange tangling of "the coming of the Lord" and the body of poor old John Brown.

Thus, in 1860-61, men of the North and of the South, each clothed in the armor of a just cause, saw no alternative to civil war. Differences had been reduced to the merits or the lack of them in Negro slavery and lifted to the level of a conflict between civilizations. Yet neither section had come to its present position through deliberate choice. The South had been reduced to the sad necessity of breaking up what Robert E. Lee called "a government inaugurated by the blood & wisdom of our patriotic fathers," and the North had been forced into the necessity of fighting to prevent it, by the despotic decrees of the emerging Modern World.

This was the culprit which had steadily pushed the sections apart and given them conflicting values. It had been responsible for the supposed injustices on the one side and the equally unjustified self-righteousness on the other. It had led the one slowly to accept consolidated nationalism, the other to fall back on states' rights; the one to accept the superiority of industrial capitalism, the other to extol the virtues of things rural-agricultural;

the one to become the champion of freedom, the other to cling to slavery.

The North had only gradually and reluctantly accepted its new capitalists, its factories, its cities, and its new communications based on steam. It had only slowly learned that the good outweighed the bad and to hail it all as progress. Only gradually had it brought its old social and moral values into line and to the support of the new day. The crusade against slavery both as an impediment to progress and as a moral blight belonged largely to the last two decades.

The South had more readily accepted the task of supplying the new age with its cotton, but it did not deliberately choose between free white labor and Negro slaves for its cotton fields. It simply took what was at hand in the mad hurry to reap profits. Virgin soils and high cotton prices only gradually silenced the harsh criticism of slavery which, up until the mid-1830's, had found wide and open expression in the Old South. Not until then was slavery called "a positive good" and the idea evolved that it constituted the foundations of a superior society.

Under such circumstances, the average Southerner really never had a fair chance to compare the merits of the old order with those of the Modern World. He met that world only as a market for cotton produced by slave labor, or as a hostile force to be resisted, not evaluated. Yet, throughout the 1850's Southern men had shown enough interest in scientific agriculture, in the building of factories, and in "the mechanic arts as the arm of civilization" to suggest that, under normal conditions, they too, in time, might have known its transforming power.

Nor did those Southerners who loved the Union and were opposed to secession ever have a fair and equal chance. Three-fourths of all those who lived at the South held no slaves and had no part in plantation life. They had shamed the North in their support of the nation at war with Mexico. They unquestionably constituted a majority in 1860. Their votes indicated as much. Yet majorities amounted to little in a period when fears, injured pride, anger, threats, and self-righteousness were involved. Under such conditions, the rabid few with emotion on their side, and with the chance to charge disloyalty, timidity, and subservience, had all the advantage. Aided by the uncompromising and haughty attitudes of Northern radicals, they reduced the majority first to silence and then to impotence. Soon the moderates found themselves moving with the tide and accepting what they knew to be disaster. We may not excuse them for their failure to act, but we can, at least, understand their feeling of helplessness in the face of what seemed to be a driving force against which resistance had all along seemed hopeless. Any assurance offered them now would indeed have seemed to be what the honest Northerner had admitted—only "base and very foolish lies."

It thus would seem that those who live a hundred years later, when the bulldozers and the factories of the Modern World are threatening to wipe out the last vestiges of the Old South, when the release of a new energy is rendering extreme nationalism a bit obsolete, when capitalism has been modified and socialized almost beyond recognition, might begin to see the sad predicament into which the Americans of 1860 had been cast by circumstances not of their own choosing or creation, and to feel sorrow for a whole people who could not avoid a bloody civil war: that they might know the futility of seeking out war guilt; that they might more clearly understand that "the world do move" and that those who do not catch stride with progress are in danger of being run over; that the old and ever-present problem of a just balance between local freedom and central efficiency cannot be solved by force—even by civil war—but must be sought in a wise and tolerant statesmanship.

Readings

Any comprehensive study of the election of 1860 is in large measure an examination into the causes of the Civil War. Lincoln's election to the presidency was the occasion which brought a decade of accumulating emotions of fear and animosity to the point of resolution. Yet historians have never agreed on the nature of those divisive forces or how and why they dragged the country from the Republican victory to a secession movement and civil war. Some writings have emphasized this perennial disagreement and with it the vast complexity of causation. In this connection the student should not overlook Thomas J. Pressly, *Americans Interpret Their Civil War* (Princeton, N.J., 1954) and the earlier essay by Howard K. Beale, "What Historians Have Said About the Causes of the Civil War," Social Science Research Council *Bulletin No. 54* (1946). Another valuable study is Pieter Geyl, "The American Civil War and the Problem of Inevitability," *New England Quarterly*, XXIV (June, 1951). Two

excellent compilations on causation also reveal the conflict in interpretation: Edwin C. Rozwenc (ed.), *The
Causes of the American Civil War* (Boston, 1961) and
Kenneth M. Stampp (ed.), *The Causes of the Civil War*
(Englewood Cliffs, N.J., 1959). Kenneth Stampp's col-
lection of readings introduces both contemporary and
later writings to illustrate seven basic interpretations of
the coming of the Civil War in America.

Perhaps the best over-all survey of sectional politics
and the party revolution of the forties and fifties is Avery
Craven, *The Coming of the Civil War* (New York, 1942;
2nd ed., Chicago, 1957). Most of his ideas have been dis-
tilled, with a somewhat heavier emphasis on economic factors, in his brief study, *Civil War in the Making 1815-1860*
(Baton Rouge, La., 1959). The most ambitious undertaking
in analyzing the coming of the war in all of its complexity
are the four volumes covering the period from 1847 to 1861
by Allan Nevins: *Ordeal of the Union* (2 vols., New York,
1947) and *The Emergence of Lincoln* (2 vols., New York,
1950). These large volumes touch all aspects of American
life; their judgments on why the Civil War came are similar
to those of Craven. A general study of considerable worth
is Wilfred E. Binkley, *American Political Parties: Their
Natural History* (New York, 1943). Chapters VIII and IX
are especially useful for a study of politics in the fifties.
Among the more valuable studies of the antislavery movement and its impact on American life and politics are
Theodore C. Smith, *The Liberty and Free Soil Parties
in the Northwest* (Cambridge, Mass., 1897); Dwight L.
Dumond, *Anti-Slavery Origins of the Civil War in the
United States* (Ann Arbor, Mich., 1939); William O.
Lynch, "Antislavery Tendencies of the Democratic Party
in the Northwest, 1848-50," *Mississippi Valley Historical*

Review, XI (December, 1924); and the new survey by Louis Filler, *The Crusade Against Slavery, 1830-1860* (New York, 1960).

Each event of the fifties which deepened sectional antagonism has been subjected to careful analysis. For a standard judgment of Douglas' motivation in the Kansas-Nebraska controversy see Frank H. Hodder's two articles, "Genesis of the Kansas-Nebraska Act," *Proceedings* of the State Historical Society of Wisconsin (1912) and "The Railroad Background of the Kansas-Nebraska Act," *Mississippi Valley Historical Review,* XII (June, 1925). Roy Frank Nichols has analyzed the pressures of Southern politicians on Douglas in "The Kansas-Nebraska Act: A Century of Historiography," *Mississippi Valley Historical Review,* XLIII (September, 1956). On the background of the Kansas-Nebraska Act is also J. C. Malin, *The Nebraska Question, 1853-1854* (Lawrence, Kan., 1953). On the impact of the Kansas-Nebraska Act on politics in the Northwest see Willard H. Smith, "Schuyler Colfax and the Political Upheaval of 1854-1855," *Mississippi Valley Historical Review,* XXVIII (December, 1941).

On the Kansas question the standard work is J. C. Malin, *John Brown and the Legend of Fifty-Six* (Philadelphia, 1942). Revealing the discrepancy between what occurred in Kansas and what Northern reporters and editors told their readers is the excellent article by Bernard A. Weisberger, "The Newspaper Reporter and the Kansas Imbroglio," *Mississippi Valley Historical Review,* XXXVI (March, 1950). On the Dred Scott case are Vincent C. Hopkins, *Dred Scott's Case* (New York, 1951) and Frank H. Hodder, "Some Phases of the Dred Scott Case," *Mississippi Valley Historical Review,* XVI (June, 1929).

Among the many studies that treat adequately the rise

of the Republican Party in the fifties are Andrew Wallace Crandall, *The Early History of the Republican Party 1854-1856* (Boston, 1930) and Malcom Moos, *The Republicans: A History of Their Party* (New York, 1956). Both books contain much useful and colorful information. Jeter A. Isely, *Horace Greeley and the Republican Party, 1853-1861: A Study of the New York Tribune* (Princeton, N.J., 1947) is an excellent monograph based on exhaustive research. Containing much information on the election of 1856 is Ruhl Jacob Bartlett, *John C. Fremont and the Republican Party* (Columbus, Ohio, 1930).

Lincoln's role in the building of the Republican Party in the late fifties has been subjected to extensive scholarship. Still the most comprehensive biography of the prepresidential Lincoln, rich in historical background, is Volume II of Albert J. Beveridge, *Abraham Lincoln, 1809-1858* (2 vols., Boston, 1928). William E. Baringer, *Lincoln's Rise to Power* (Boston, 1937) takes up where Beveridge leaves off and carries Lincoln's career through the nomination for the presidency in 1860. Also by the same author is the useful *Lincoln Day by Day, a Chronology* (2 vols., Washington, D.C., 1960). Volume I of James G. Randall, *Lincoln the President, Springfield to Gettysburg* (2 vols., New York, 1945) contains a scholarly treatment of Lincoln's rise to the presidency, as do the two outstanding one-volume biographies of Lincoln: Benjamin P. Thomas, *Abraham Lincoln, a Biography* (New York, 1952) and the more recent Reinhard H. Luthin, *The Real Abraham Lincoln* (Englewood Cliffs, N.J., 1960).

Among the more important works dealing with specific phases of Lincoln's rise to power are Paul Angle (ed.), *Created Equal? The Complete Lincoln-Douglas Debates*

of 1858 (Chicago, 1958) and two articles by Don E. Fehrenbacher, "The Origins and Purpose of Lincoln's 'House-
Divided' Speech," *Mississippi Valley Historical Review,*
XLVI (March, 1960) and "The Nomination of Lincoln in
1858," *Abraham Lincoln Quarterly,* VI (March, 1950).
Harry V. Jaffa and Robert W. Johannsen have edited the
speeches of Lincoln and Douglas delivered on their tours
of Ohio in 1859 under the title of *In the Name of the
People: The Speeches and Writings of Lincoln and Doug-
las in the Ohio Campaign of 1859* (Columbus, Ohio, 1959).
Two recent books on Lincoln's nomination are Melvin L.
Hayes, *Mr. Lincoln Runs for President* (New York, 1960)
and Willard L. King, *Lincoln's Manager: David Davis*
(Cambridge, Mass., 1960).

Roy Frank Nichols has written the best account of the
developments which led up to the breakup of the Demo-
cratic Party at Charleston in his *The Disruption of
American Democracy* (New York, 1948). Two biographies
of Douglas which contain much useful information on
Douglas in the crisis of 1860 are George Fort Milton, *The
Eve of Conflict: Stephen A. Douglas and the Needless
War* (Boston, 1934) and Gerald Capers, *Stephen A.
Douglas: Defender of the Union* (Boston, 1959). Two perceptive articles on Douglas' popular sovereignty views
have been written by Robert W. Johannsen, "Stephen
A. Douglas, 'Harper's Magazine,' and Popular Sovereignty," *Mississippi Valley Historical Review,* XLV
(March, 1959) and "Stephen A. Douglas, Popular Sovereignty and the Territories," *Historian,* XXII (August,
1960). An invaluable account of the proceedings of all
the 1860 nominating conventions, written by a reporter
of a Cincinnati newspaper, is Murat Halstead's *Caucuses*

of 1860: A History of the National Political Conventions of the Current Presidential Campaign . . . (Columbus, Ohio, 1860). Halstead's account has been edited and republished recently by William B. Hesseltine in *Three Against Lincoln: Murat Halstead Reports the Caucuses of 1860* (Baton Rouge, La., 1960).

The standard, although old and partially outmoded, study of the campaign of 1860 is Emerson D. Fite, *The Presidential Campaign of 1860* (New York, 1911). A detailed and scholarly analysis of the Republican campaign can be found in Reinhard H. Luthin, *The First Lincoln Campaign* (Cambridge, Mass., 1944). Joseph H. Parks, *John Bell of Tennessee* (Baton Rouge, La., 1950) relates many details on the activities of the Constitutional Union Party in 1860. A valuable account of Southern participation in the 1860 campaign can be found in Ollinger Crenshaw, *The Slave States in the Presidential Election of 1860* (Baltimore, Md., 1945). A less detailed but perceptive account of the South in the campaign of 1860 can be found in Avery Craven, *The Growth of Southern Nationalism, 1848-1861* (Baton Rouge, La., 1953).

Two articles which debate the central question of the campaign of 1860 are Arthur C. Cole, "Lincoln's Election an Immediate Menace to Slavery in the States?" *American Historical Review*, XXXVI (July, 1931) and James G. deRoulhac Hamilton, "Lincoln's Election an Immediate Menace to Slavery in the States?" *American Historical Review*, XXXVII (July, 1932).

Historians have studied the secession crisis of 1860-61 in great detail. From the viewpoint of the North, the two standard volumes are David M. Potter, *Lincoln and His Party in the Secession Crisis* (New Haven, Conn.,

1942) and Kenneth M. Stampp, *And the War Came: The North in the Secession Crisis* (Baton Rouge, La., 1950). Also of value is William E. Baringer, *A House Dividing: Lincoln as President-Elect* (Springfield, Ill., 1945). On the South in the secession crisis is Dwight L. Dumond, *The Secession Movement, 1860-1861* (New York, 1931) and by the same author, *Southern Editorials on Secession* (New York, 1931). Also on the secession theme is U. B. Phillips, *The Course of the South to Secession* (New York, 1939). Three biographies of leaders of the secession movement are John W. DuBose, *The Life and Times of William Lowndes Yancey* (Birmingham, Ala., 1892), Laura A. White, *Robert Barnwell Rhett, Father of Secession* (New York, 1931), and Avery Craven, *Edmund Ruffin: Southerner* (New York, 1932). The dilemma of Northern business in the crisis is seen in P. S. Foner, *Business and Slavery: The New York Merchants and the Irrepressible Conflict* (Chapel Hill, N.C., 1941), as well as the diary of a New York lawyer in Allan Nevins and Milton H. Thomas (eds.), *The Diary of George Templeton Strong* (4 vols., New York, 1952).

Index